I0413126

Seepage Investigations of the Rio Grande from Below Leasburg Dam, Leasburg, New Mexico, to Above American Dam, El Paso, Texas, 2006–13

Open-File Report 2013–1233

U.S. Department of the Interior
U.S. Geological Survey

Seepage Investigations of the Rio Grande from Below Leasburg Dam, Leasburg, New Mexico, to Above American Dam, El Paso, Texas, 2006–13

By D.M. Crilley, A.M. Matherne, Nicole Thomas, and S.E. Falk

Open-File Report 2013–1233

U.S. Department of the Interior
U.S. Geological Survey

U.S. Department of the Interior
SALLY JEWELL, Secretary

U.S. Geological Survey
Suzette M. Kimball, Acting Director

U.S. Geological Survey, Reston, Virginia: 2013

For more information on the USGS—the Federal source for science about the Earth, its natural and living resources, natural hazards, and the environment, visit http://www.usgs.gov or call 1–888–ASK–USGS.

For an overview of USGS information products, including maps, imagery, and publications, visit http://www.usgs.gov/pubprod

To order this and other USGS information products, visit http://store.usgs.gov

Suggested citation:
Crilley, D.M., Matherne, A.M., Thomas, Nicole, and Falk, S.E., 2013, Seepage investigations of the Rio Grande from below Leasburg Dam, Leasburg, New Mexico, to above American Dam, El Paso, Texas, 2006–13: U.S. Geological Survey Open-File Report 2013–1233, 34 p., http://pubs.usgs.gov/of/2013/1233/.

Acknowledgments

A special acknowledgment is due to Edward "Nick" Nickerson, retired U.S. Geological Survey hydrologist, for his leadership and management of this project from 1988 to 2012. Nick's dedication to the collection of relevant high-quality data for this project and for the Mesilla Basin monitoring program has been an important contribution to advancing the scientific understanding of the complex hydrology of the Mesilla Basin. The authors also gratefully acknowledge the City of Las Cruces Utilities, Elephant Butte Irrigation District, El Paso Water Utilities (2006), International Boundary and Water Commission–U.S. Section, New Mexico Environment Department, New Mexico Interstate Stream Commission, New Mexico Office of the State Engineer, New Mexico State University, and U.S. Bureau of Reclamation for their cooperation and support of this project.

Contents

Figures

Tables

Conversion Factors

Inch/Pound to SI

Multiply	By	To obtain
Length		
inch (in.)	2.54	centimeter (cm)
inch (in.)	25.4	millimeter (mm)
mile (mi)	1.609	kilometer (km)
Flow rate		
foot per second (ft/s)	0.3048	meter per second (m/s)

Temperature in degrees Celsius (°C) may be converted to degrees Fahrenheit (°F) as follows:

°F=(1.8×°C)+32

Temperature in degrees Fahrenheit (°F) may be converted to degrees Celsius (°C) as follows:

°C=(°F-32)/1.8

Specific conductance is given in microsiemens per centimeter at 25 degrees Celsius (μS/cm at 25°C).

Seepage Investigations of the Rio Grande from Below Leasburg Dam, Leasburg, New Mexico, to Above American Dam, El Paso, Texas, 2006–13

By D.M. Crilley, A.M. Matherne, Nicole Thomas, and S.E. Falk

Abstract

Seepage investigations were conducted annually by the U.S. Geological Survey from 1988 to 1998 and from 2004 to 2013 along a 64-mile reach of the Rio Grande from below Leasburg Dam, Leasburg, New Mexico, to above American Dam, El Paso, Texas, as part of the Mesilla Basin monitoring program. Results of studies conducted from 2006 to 2013 are presented in this report. Seepage investigations were conducted over a period of 1–2 days in February of each year, during low-flow conditions in the non-irrigation season. During the seepage investigations, discharge was measured at as many as 24 sites along the Rio Grande and as many as 20 inflow sites within the study reach.

Net seepage gain or loss was computed for each subreach by subtracting the discharge measured at the upstream location from the discharge measured at the closest downstream location along the river and then subtracting any inflow to the river within the subreach. An estimated gain or loss was determined to be significant when it exceeded the cumulative measurement uncertainty associated with the net seepage computation. Study reaches during 2006 to 2013 ranged from 20.2 to 64 miles in length, and seepage losses ranged from 8.2 ± 3.1 to 47.9 ± 8.2 cubic feet per second.

Introduction

Increasing water demand within the Mesilla Basin and adjacent areas (fig. 1) has resulted in increased groundwater withdrawals in the basin. In 1987, the U.S. Geological Survey (USGS) established the Mesilla Basin Monitoring Program (http://nm.water.usgs.gov/projects/mesilla) to document and identify trends in groundwater conditions and stream/aquifer relations. The monitoring program has continued through the present (2013) in cooperation with the City of Las Cruces Utilities, Elephant Butte Irrigation District, El Paso Water Utilities (2006), International Boundary and Water Commission–U.S. Section, New Mexico Environment Department, New Mexico Interstate Stream Commission, New Mexico Office of the State Engineer, New Mexico State University, and U.S. Bureau of Reclamation.

Seepage investigations on the Rio Grande from below Leasburg Dam, Leasburg, New Mexico, to above American Dam, El Paso, Texas, have been a component of the monitoring program since 1988. Seepage gain or loss is the slow interstitial movement of water into or out of a body of surface or subsurface water (U.S. Geological Survey, 2013). Information on seepage gains or losses in the Rio Grande is important to water managers in the Mesilla Basin, where multiple water users rely on surface water in a highly interconnected hydrogeologic basin (Moyer and others, 2013). Results of seepage investigations on the Rio Grande conducted annually by the USGS from 1988 to 1998 and from 2004 to 2005 as part of the Mesilla Basin monitoring program were published in USGS annual water-data reports, available at http://nm.water.usgs.gov/publications/pubswdr.html.

Purpose and Scope

This report describes the methods used to obtain discharge measurements and presents the results of seepage investigations conducted along the Rio Grande from below Leasburg Dam, Leasburg, N. Mex., to above American Dam, El Paso, Tex. (hereafter referred to as the "study reach"), from 2006 to 2013. Discharge measurements for as many as 24 river sites and 20 inflow sites are presented for each annual seepage investigation. Net seepage gain to or loss from the river, computed on the basis of discharge measurements for as many as 22 subreaches within the study reach, is presented. Field measurements and observations recorded at measurement locations are compiled in appendix 1, along with associated water temperature, specific conductance, discharge, discharge-measurement type, discharge rating, and remarks on streamflow and channel conditions.

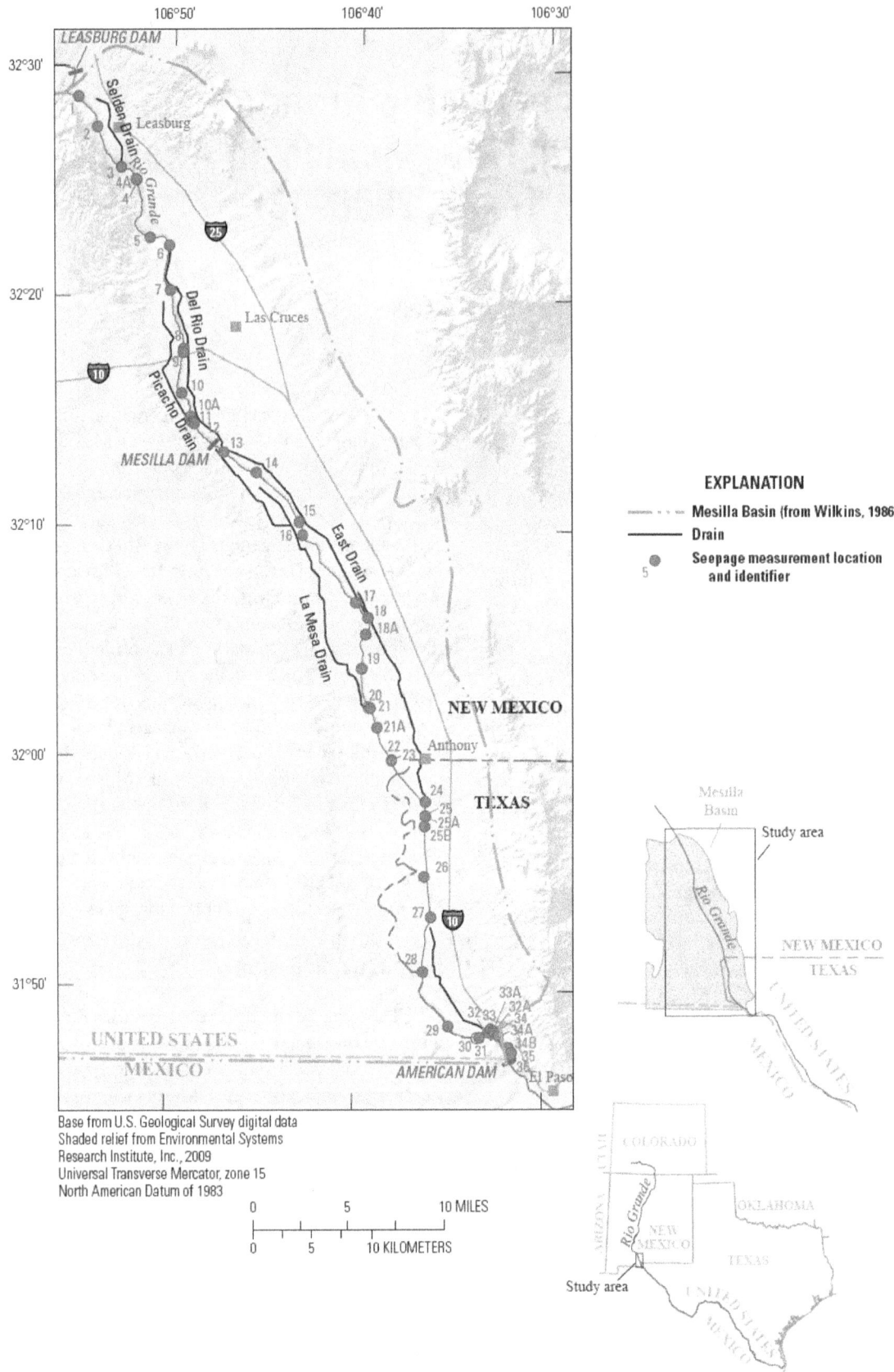

Figure 1. U.S. Geological Survey Rio Grande seepage investigation measurement locations from below Leasburg Dam, Leasburg, New Mexico, to above American Dam, El Paso, Texas, 2006–13.

Description of Study Reach and Measurement Locations

The study reach was a 64-mile section of the Rio Grande from below Leasburg Dam, Leasburg, N. Mex., to above American Dam, El Paso, Tex. Measurement locations followed those established in previous seepage investigations (1988–98 and 2004–5) (figs. 1 and 2, table 1), with modifications to accommodate site-specific conditions as noted in the description of the seepage investigation for each year. Sites included locations along the river and at points of inflow to the river; points of outflow from the river were not included because no diversions occurred within the study reach during the seepage investigations. The USGS station identification and station name associated with each measurement location site identification are given in table 1. River miles are referenced upstream from the Rio Grande confluence with the Gulf of Mexico; for example, site 34, Rio Grande at El Paso, Tex., is designated as river mile 1,249.9 (Hendricks, 1964). The relative locations of measurement sites are shown in figure 2, and associated river miles are given in table 1. Measurement locations in any year included as many as 24 river sites and as many as 20 inflow sites.

Inflows to the river included municipal and industrial discharge of effluent, agricultural drains, water from reservoirs, and discharge of water from other sources. Outfall from wastewater treatment plants (WWTPs) discharged to the river at six locations (sites 9, 18A, 21A, 30, 32A, and 35) at river miles 1,295.4; 1,275.7; 1,270.5; 1,250.9; 1,250.2; and 1,248.4, respectively. Drains, which collect groundwater return flow at locations where the water table is at a higher elevation than the bottom of the river channel, discharged to the river at sites 3, 6, 11, 15, 18, 20, 24, and 32 at river miles 1,307.6; 1,301.2; 1,291.8; 1,283.6; 1,276.6; 1,271.6; 1,265.4; and 1,250.3, respectively. Water from Keystone Reservoir, El Paso, Tex. (site 33), entered the river at river mile 1,250.1. Inflows from other sources included storm water inflows, unspecified pipe inflows, seeps, a temporary well used to dewater a construction area, and other sources within the study reach. These inflows (sites 23, 25C, 33A, 34A, and 34B) entered the study reach at river miles 1,268.4; 1,264.7; 1,250.0; 1,249.7; and 1,248.7, respectively.

Methods

General Approach

Seepage investigations were conducted over a period of 1–2 days in February of each year, during low-flow conditions in the non-irrigation season. During the seepage investigations, discharge was measured at sites along the river and at locations where inflows to the river occurred. Outflows from the river did not occur during the seepage investigations; the outflow term is retained in the presentation of seepage computation equations, however, for completeness of discussion. Discharge measurements were collected over an approximate 7-hour period beginning at about 9 a m. and ending about 4 p m. Net seepage gain or loss was computed for each subreach by subtracting the discharge measured at the upstream location from the discharge measured at the closest downstream location along the river and then subtracting any inflow to the river within the subreach. A subreach is defined as the interval between two adjacent measurement locations along the river. Inflows to the river were considered contributions and not seepage gains. Seepage gain or loss was considered to be meaningful for subreaches where the computed net seepage gain or loss exceeded the cumulative measurement uncertainty for the computation (see section "Seepage Computation").

Gains or losses in discharge to the Rio Grande can result from seepage in the streambed or from bank storage, evaporation from the water surface, and transpiration by vegetation along the river banks. Discharge in this reach of the Rio Grande is largely controlled by irrigation releases from Elephant Butte Dam, located on the Rio Grande about 70 miles upstream from Leasburg (Moyer and others, 2013). Irrigation releases occur during March through October of each year. Streamflow in this reach of the Rio Grande during the non-irrigation season is low and steady, relative to streamflow during irrigation season, and contributions to streamflow due to bank storage were considered minimal. Average air temperature during the 2006–13 seepage investigations was about 50 degrees Fahrenheit (10 degrees Celsius; National Climatic Data Center, 2013). Seepage investigations were conducted during February of each year when losses due to evaporation from the water surface and transpiration by vegetation are considered minimal relative to summer levels. Because the effects of bank storage, evaporation, and transpiration on streamflow at this time of year are considered minimal, computed gains or losses in discharge for the seepage investigations presented in this report are assumed to be due to seepage to or from the streambed resulting from the interchange of surface water and groundwater.

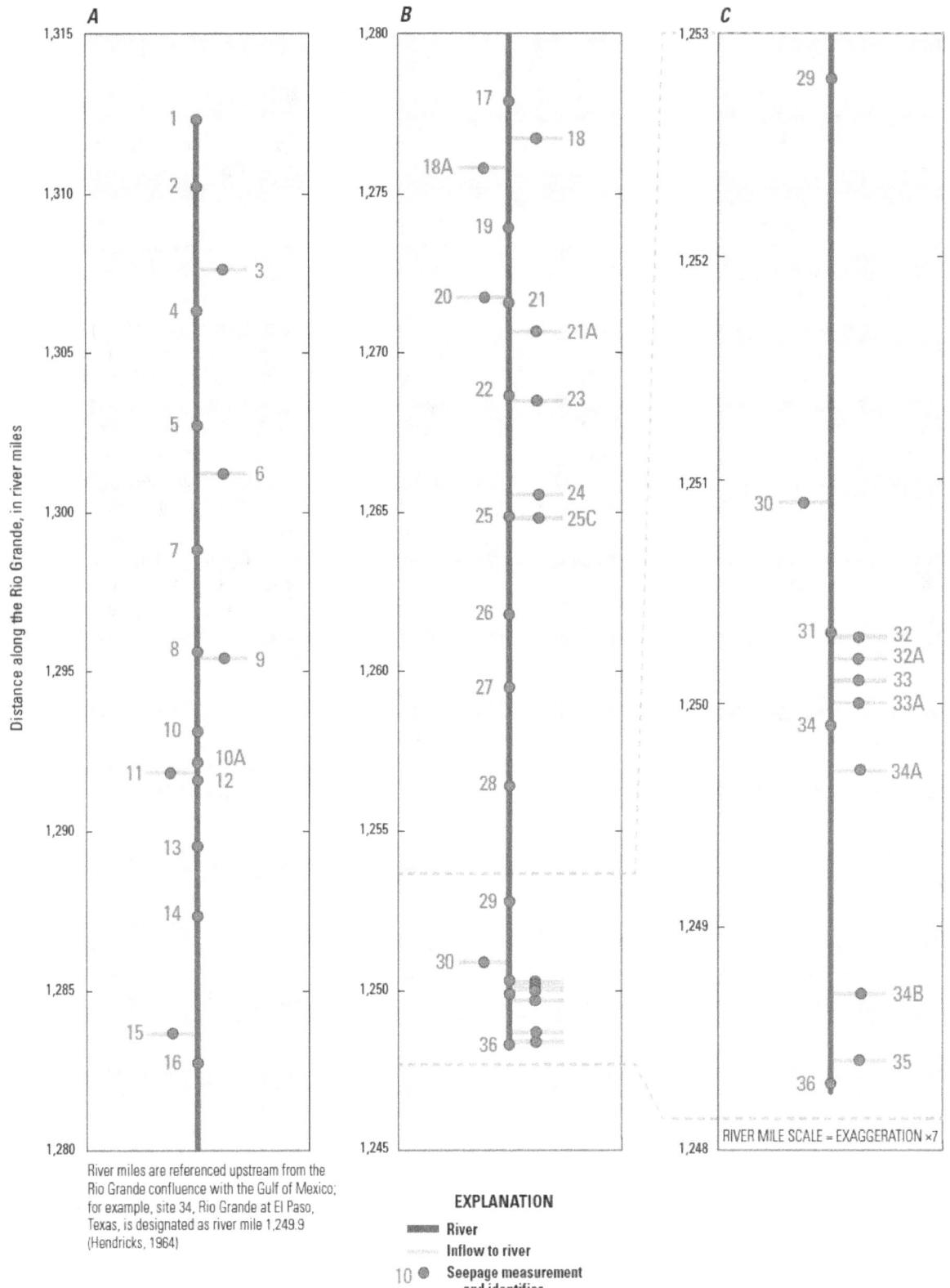

Figure 2. Schematic showing U.S. Geological Survey Rio Grande seepage investigation measurement locations from below Leasburg Dam, Leasburg, New Mexico, to above American Dam, El Paso, Texas, 2006–13, and the relation of inflows to the river within the study reach. *A*, Location of measurement sites 1–16. *B*, Location of measurement sites 17–36. *C*, An expanded view of the location of measurement sites 29–36.

Table 1. Location of U.S. Geological Survey Rio Grande seepage investigation measurements from below Leasburg Dam, Leasburg, New Mexico, to above American Dam, El Paso, Texas, 2006–13.

[ID, identification; USGS, U.S. Geological Survey; NAD 27, North American Datum of 1927; NM, New Mexico; WWTP, wastewater treatment plant; TX, Texas]

Site ID (see fig. 1)	USGS station ID	Station name	Latitude (NAD 27)	Longitude (NAD 27)	River mile[1]	Years of site inclusion in seepage investigation during 2006–13
1	322841106551010	Rio Grande below Leasburg Dam, NM	32.4769	-106.9197	1,312.3	2006–9, 2012–13
2	322721106540810	Rio Grande near Leasburg, NM	32.4544	-106.9017	1,310.2	2006–9, 2012–13
3	322541106525110	Selden Drain at Levee Road near Leasburg, NM	32.4281	-106.8814	1,307.6	2006–9, 2012–13
4	322505106520110	Rio Grande near Hill, NM	32.4186	-106.8672	1,306.3	2006–9, 2012–13
5	322234106511710	Rio Grande at Shalem Bridge near Dona Ana, NM	32.3762	-106.8553	1,302.7	2006–9, 2012–13
6	322214106501410	Spillway Number 5 near Dona Ana, NM	32.3703	-106.8381	1,301.2	2006–9, 2012–13
7	322018106500910	Rio Grande near Picacho, NM	32.3383	-106.8367	1,298.8	2006–9, 2012–13
8	321745106492510	Rio Grande below Picacho Bridge near Las Cruces, NM	32.2964	-106.8242	1,295.6	2006–9, 2012–13
9	321735106492610	Las Cruces WWTP Outfall, Las Cruces, NM	32.2928	-106.8247	1,295.4	2006–9, 2012–13
10	321549106492910	Rio Grande at NM-359 Bridge near Mesilla, NM	32.2637	-106.8253	1,293.1	2006–9, 2012–13
10A	321448106490010	Rio Grande above Picacho Drain, NM	32.2468	-106.8172	1,292.0	2006
11	321434106485610	Picacho Drain above Mesilla Dam,NM	32.2422	-106.8153	1,291.8	2006–9, 2012–13
12	321430106484910	Rio Grande below Picacho Drain, NM	32.2419	-106.8142	1,291.7	2006–9, 2012–13
13	321317106471510	Rio Grande below Mesilla Dam near Santo Tomas, NM	32.2211	-106.7886	1,289.5	2006–9, 2012–13
14	321224106453210	Rio Grande at NM-28 Bridge near San Pablo, NM	32.2067	-106.7597	1,287.3	2006–9, 2012–13
15	321014106431410	Santo Tomas River Drain at Levee Road near San Miguel, NM	32.1707	-106.7211	1,283.6	2006–9, 2012–13
16	320943106425810	Rio Grande NM-192 Bridge near San Miguel, NM	32.1620	-106.7167	1,282.7	2006–9, 2012–13
17	320648106400510	Rio Grande at NM-189 Bridge near Vado, NM	32.1136	-106.6689	1,277.8	2006–9, 2012–13
18	320610106393110	Del Rio Drain at Levee Road near Vado, NM	32.1029	-106.6592	1,276.6	2006–9, 2012–13
18A	320525106393410	Dona Ana Co South Central WWTP Outfall near Vado, NM	32.0903	-106.6600	1,275.7	2006–9, 2012–13
19	320356106394510	Rio Grande at NM-226 Bridge near Berino, NM	32.0656	-106.6633	1,273.8	2006–9, 2012–13
20	320214106392510	La Mesa Drain at LeveeRoad near Chamberino, NM	32.0373	-106.6575	1,271.6	2006–9, 2012–13
21	320212106391810	Rio Grande below La Mesa Drain near Chamberino, NM	32.0369	-106.6561	1,271.5	2006–9, 2012–13

Table 1. Location of U.S. Geological Survey Rio Grande seepage investigation measurements from below Leasburg Dam, Leasburg, New Mexico, to above American Dam, El Paso, Texas, 2006–13.—Continued

[ID, identification; USGS, U.S. Geological Survey; NAD 27, North American Datum of 1927; NM, New Mexico; WWTP, wastewater treatment plant; TX, Texas]

Site ID (see fig. 1)	USGS station ID	Station name	Latitude (NAD 27)	Longitude (NAD 27)	River mile[1]	Years of site inclusion in seepage investigation during 2006–13
21A	320122106385610	Anthony WWTP Outfall at NM-186 Bridge near Anthony, NM	32.0228	-106.6489	1,270.5	2009, 2012–13
22	315958106380710	Rio Grande at NM-225 Bridge near Anthony, NM	31.9994	-106.6361	1,268.5	2006–13
23	315957106380610	Pipe Inflow at NM-225 Bridge near Anthony, NM	31.9992	-106.6353	1,268.4	2006–13
24	315807106361910	East Side Drain at Levee Road near Anthony, TX	31.9687	-106.6058	1,265.4	2006–13
25	315733106361610	Rio Grande at Vinton Bridge near Vinton, TX	31.9594	-106.6050	1,264.7	2006–13
25C	315652106361710	Temporary Well-C Inflow below Vinton Bridge, near Vinton, TX	31.9479	-106.6053	1,264.7	2006
26	315454106360610	Rio Grande at TX-259 Bridge, Canutillo, TX	31.9153	-106.6022	1,261.6	2006–13
27	315309106355510	Rio Grande at Borderland Bridge near Borderland, TX	31.8861	-106.5989	1,259.3	2006–13
28	315046106361810	Rio Grande at TX-260 Bridge near Santa Teresa, NM	31.8464	-106.6058	1,256.2	2006–13
29	314824106345710	Rio Grande near Sunland Park, NM	31.8067	-106.5828	1,252.8	2006–13
30	314755106332510	Sunland Park WWTP Outfall, Sunland Park, NM	31.7986	-106.5575	1,250.9	2006–13
31	314756106331610	Rio Grande at Sunland Park Bridge, Sunland Park, NM	31.7989	-106.5550	1,250.3	2006–13
32	314810106324610	Montoya Drain at Sunland Park, NM	31.8029	-106.5467	1,250.3	2006–13
32A	314812106324410	El Paso Electric Plant Wastewater Outfall, Sunland Park, NM	31.8036	-106.5461	1,250.2	2006–13
33	314818106323910	Keystone Reservoir Inlet, El Paso, TX	31.8050	-106.5444	1,250.1	2006–13
33A	314813106322810	Side-Channel Inlet above Courchesne Bridge, El Paso, TX	31.8036	-106.5417	1,250.0	2006–13
34	08364000	Rio Grande at El Paso, TX	31.8029	-106.5408	1,249.9	2006–13
34A	314802106321710	Side-Channel Inlet below Courchesne Bridge, El Paso, TX	31.8007	-106.5386	1,249.7	2006–13
34B	314731106314510	Side-Channel Inflow above Executive Blvd, El Paso, TX	31.7921	-106.5297	1,248.7	2010
35	314718106313410	El Paso Water Utility Northwest WWTP Outfall, El Paso, TX	31.7884	-106.5267	1,248.4	2010–13
36	314713106313610	Rio Grande above American Dam, El Paso, TX	31.7871	-106.5272	1,248.3	2010–13

[1]River miles are referenced upstream from the Rio Grande confluence with the Gulf of Mexico; for example, site 34, Rio Grande at El Paso, Tex., is designated as river mile 1,249.9 (Hendricks, 1964).

Data Collection

Measurement of Surface-Water Discharge

Discharge measurements used for the seepage investigations were collected by USGS personnel using a variety of measurement techniques, depending on site characteristics, or were as reported from other sources. Instantaneous discharge was measured by using an Acoustic Doppler Velocimeter (ADV) or a portable 3-inch Parshall flume (standard USGS protocols as described in Rantz and others, 1982; Kilpatrick and Schneider, 1983; Nolan and Shields, 2000; Oberg and others, 2005; Turnipseed and Sauer, 2010). In general, 25–30 vertical measurements were made at a cross section, with spacing such that no partial section contained more than 5 percent of the total cross-sectional discharge. A Parshall flume was used when surface-water depths were too shallow and velocities were too low to measure discharge by using an ADV (Kilpatrick and Schneider, 1983). Discharge measurements were reported in cubic feet per second (ft³/s) and assigned a qualitative accuracy rating, on the basis of a field assessment of discharge measurement and channel conditions, of excellent (less than or equal to 2 percent), good (less than or equal to 5 percent), fair (less than or equal to 8 percent), or poor (greater than 8 percent) (Turnipseed and Sauer, 2010) (app. 1).

Effluent from municipal and industrial WWTPs discharged to the river in one of three ways: (1) as a discrete variable-flow (batch) release, (2) as a continuous equalized-flow (equalized) release, or (3) as a continuous variable-flow (unequalized) release. Discharge from a WWTP was reported as either the instantaneous discharge metered by the plant at a specific time (Reported-I) or as the mean daily discharge computed from the total discharge for the day metered by the plant (Reported-MDI) (app. 1); these two discharge measurements can be substantially different for WWTPs that batch release effluent. For the six WWTPs that discharged effluent to the river (sites 9, 18A, 21A, 30, 32A, and 35), the most appropriate method of reporting discharge and the associated uncertainty in the reported measurement was assessed on a site-by-site basis. The assessment was based on the way in which effluent was released from the plant and on the percentage difference between the Reported-I discharge and the Reported-MDI discharge for that day. Of the 6 WWTPs included in the seepage investigation, 2 were batch-release plants (sites 18A and 32A), 1 was an equalized-release plant (site 9), and 3 were unequalized-release plants (sites 21A, 30, and 35). Prior to 2009, site 21A was not included in seepage investigations because effluent from the WWTP discharged to a nearby drain rather than to the Rio Grande. Discharge data for sites 18A and 32A are designated as Reported-MDI with a measurement uncertainty greater than or equal to 10 percent. Discharge data for sites 9, 21A, and 30 are designated as Reported-I with a measurement uncertainty less than or equal to 8 percent. Discharge of plant effluent at site 35 was measured at the riverside outfall and assigned a

measurement uncertainty of less than or equal to 8 percent on the basis of the continuous but unequalized release of discharge from the plant. Although not a WWTP, the discharge at site 25C, a temporary well used to dewater a construction area, was classified as Reported-MDI with a measurement uncertainty greater than or equal to 10 percent.

Measurement of Surface-Water Quality

Water-quality samples were collected at selected sites during the seepage investigations by using USGS collection protocols for water-quality samples and the USGS equal-width increment (EWI) sampling method where applicable (U.S. Geological Survey, 2006). Field parameters were measured with multiparameter water-quality meters calibrated according to standard USGS protocols (Wilde and Radtke, variously dated). Field determinations at the water-quality sites included specific conductance, temperature, pH, and dissolved oxygen. Laboratory determinations included the analysis of total dissolved solids and selected ion concentrations. A discussion of the water-quality data is beyond the scope of this report, but water-quality data for samples analyzed by the USGS National Water Quality Laboratory in Denver, Colorado, from selected seepage investigation sites can be accessed at http://qwwebservices.usgs.gov/.

Seepage Computation

Computations presented as part of the seepage investigations include net seepage gain or loss, estimation of uncertainty for each measurement, and significance of the computed net seepage gain or loss.

Net Seepage Gain or Loss

The mass balance equation used for calculating net seepage gain or loss in a subreach is as follows (Simonds and Sinclair, 2002):

$$Q_S = Q_{ds} - Q_{us} - Q_{in} + Q_{out} \qquad (1)$$

where

Q_S is the net seepage gain or loss for a subreach, in cubic feet per second;

Q_{ds} is the discharge measured at the downstream end of the subreach, in cubic feet per second;

Q_{us} is the discharge measured at the upstream end of the subreach, in cubic feet per second;

Q_{in} is the sum of inflows, in cubic feet per second; and

Q_{out} is the sum of outflows, in cubic feet per second.

The result is the estimated net flux of water gained or lost from the streambed for the subreach. If Q_{ds} is less than Q_{us} plus

Q_{in}—that is, if less discharge was measured at the downstream section of the subreach than was measured at the upstream section plus any inflow to that subreach (equation 1)—then the algebraic sign of the net seepage is negative (-),which signifies a loss in discharge for the subreach. Conversely, if Q_{ds} is greater than Q_{us} plus Q_{in}, then the algebraic sign of the net seepage is positive (+), which signifies a gain in discharge for that subreach. Q_{out} was zero in the calculations for all years included in this report because no diversions or outflows occurred within the study reach during the seepage investigations. For example, in the 2006 seepage investigation (table 2), the net seepage gain or loss for the subreach "8 to 10" was computed as -8.0 ft³/s (Q_S), which is the difference between the measured discharge of 10.7 ft³/s at site 10 (Q_{ds}) and the measured discharge of 0.144 ft³/s at site 8 (Q_{us}), minus the measured inflow of 18.6 ft³/s at site 9 (Q_{in}).

Estimation of Uncertainty

Individual discharge measurements were assigned a qualitative accuracy rating that represents the percentage of uncertainty in an individual measurement and was based on a subjective evaluation of the measurement made by the hydrographer on the basis of multiple factors that could affect the quality of the measurement (Sauer and Meyer, 1992). These factors include the instrumentation used, number and distribution of vertical sections where velocity is measured, estimation of average velocity, uniformity of streamflow, regularity and firmness of channel bottom, steadiness of stage and discharge during the measurement, and presence or absence of ice, wind, or debris in the streamflow that could affect the ability of the current meter to accurately measure the current velocity (Wilberg and Stolp, 2005). The uncertainty in the measurement of discharge was assigned a numerical value, derived from the qualitative accuracy rating, as follows: excellent, 2 percent; good, 5 percent; fair, 8 percent; and poor, 10 percent. If there was no measurable discharge at a site, then the uncertainty for the individual measurement was zero and the individual uncertainty did not contribute numerically to the cumulative uncertainty estimation of the seepage computation for the subreach.

The cumulative uncertainty estimation associated with the computed net seepage gain or loss for a subreach was determined by using the following equation modified from Wheeler and Eddy-Miller (2005):

$$\delta Q_s = \sqrt{\left(a_1 Q_1\right)^2 + \left(a_2 Q_2\right)^2 \ldots + \left(a_n Q_n\right)^2} \qquad (2)$$

where

δQ_s is the cumulative uncertainty in the computation of net seepage gain or loss, in cubic feet per second;

a_n is the uncertainty of a measurement, in percent; and

Q_n is the measured discharge, in cubic feet per second.

For example, in the 2006 seepage investigation (table 2), the measurement uncertainty of the individual discharge measurement for site 8 was plus or minus (±) 0.003 ft³/s ($a_1 Q_1$), computed as the product of the discharge measurement of 0.144 ft³/s (Q_1) and the discharge-measurement accuracy rating of 2 percent (a_1). The cumulative measurement uncertainty associated with the net seepage gain or loss for the subreach "8 to 10" was ± 1.6 ft³/s (δQ_s), computed as the square root of the sum of the squares of the measurement uncertainties for site 8, ± 0.003 ft³/s ($a_1 Q_1$); site 9, ± 1.5 ft³/s ($a_2 Q_2$); and site 10, ± 0.5 ft³/s ($a_3 Q_3$).

Significance of Seepage Gain or Loss

Shallow water depths and poor channel conditions, particularly during dry years, can result in increased uncertainties (exceeding 8 percent) in the computation of net seepage gains and losses. In some cases, the cumulative measurement uncertainty can exceed the net seepage gain or loss computed for a subreach. An estimated gain or loss was determined to be meaningful when it exceeded the cumulative measurement uncertainty associated with the net seepage computation. For the determination of significance, the net seepage gain or loss and the cumulative measurement uncertainty were normalized to allow for comparison between subreaches with varying discharges and for a particular subreach in different years. The percentage of normalized seepage gain or loss and normalized cumulative uncertainty was computed for each subreach by using the following equations modified from Wilberg and Stolp (2005):

$$N_d = \left| \frac{Q_S}{MaxQ_{\left[(Q_{us}+Q_{in}),\,(Q_{ds}+Q_{out})\right]}} \right| \times 100 \qquad (3)$$

where

N_d is the absolute value of the percentage of normalized seepage difference, and

$MaxQ$ is the maximum discharge measured along a subreach as either the downstream discharge plus any outflow or the upstream discharge plus any inflow, in cubic feet per second.

$$N_e = \left| \frac{\delta Q_s}{MaxQ_{\left[(Q_{us}+Q_{in}),\,(Q_{ds}+Q_{out})\right]}} \right| \times 100 \qquad (4)$$

where

N_e is the absolute value of the percentage of normalized cumulative uncertainty.

Table 2. Summary of measured discharge and the computed net seepage gain or loss in streamflow along river subreaches, Rio Grande seepage investigation, February 14–15, 2006.

[Site number: see table 1 and figures 1 and 2 for locations of sites; Q_{us}, discharge measured at upstream river channel site; ft³/s, cubic foot per second; ±, plus or minus; Q_{in}, discharge measured at inflow site (individual subreaches had between 0 and 4 inflows; subscript number indicates inflow site 1, 2, 3, or 4, ordered upstream to downstream); Q_{ds}, discharge measured at downstream river channel site; Q_s, net seepage gain or loss. See text for equations, description of cumulative uncertainty computation, and definitions of terms; $N_d\%$, normalized percentage difference, used to determine the difference between discharge measured at upstream and downstream sites of a given subreach. $N_e\%$, normalized percentage error, used to determine if a computed gain or loss exceeds errors associated with discharge measurement; ≥, greater than or equal to; Y, yes; N, no; %, percent; —, not applicable]

Subreach[1]	Sites included in subreach[1]	Distance (miles)	Sample date	Q_{us} with percentage measurement uncertainty in parentheses (ft³/s)	Q_{in1} with percentage of measurement uncertainty in parentheses (ft³/s)	Q_{in2} with percentage of measurement uncertainty in parentheses (ft³/s)	Q_{in3} with percentage of measurement uncertainty in parentheses (ft³/s)	Q_{in4} with percentage of measurement uncertainty in parentheses (ft³/s)	Q_{ds} with percentage of measurement uncertainty in parentheses (ft³/s)	Q_s (ft³/s)	Normalized percentage difference ($N_d\%$)	Normalized percentage error ($N_e\%$)	$N_d\% \geq N_e\%$ (Y or N)
1 to 2	1, 2	2.1	2/14/2006	6.67 (5%)	—	—	—	—	6.92 (5%)	0.25 ± 0.48	4	7	N
2 to 4	2, 3, 4	3.9	2/14/2006	6.92 (5%)	0 (0%)	—	—	—	11.1 (5%)	4.2 ± 0.7	38	6	Y
4 to 5	4, 5	3.6	2/14/2006	11.1 (5%)	—	—	—	—	8.65 (5%)	-2.5 ± 0.7	22	6	Y
5 to 7	5, 6, 7	3.9	2/14/2006	8.65 (5%)	0 (0%)	—	—	—	5.57 (5%)	-3.08 ± 0.51	36	6	Y
7 to 8	7, 8	3.2	2/14/2006	5.57 (5%)	—	—	—	—	0.144 (2%)	-5.43 ± 0.28	97	5	Y
8 to 10	8, 9, 10	2.5	2/14/2006	0.144 (2%)	18.5 (8%)	—	—	—	10.7 (5%)	-8.0 ± 1.6	43	8	Y
10 to 10A	10, 10A	1.1	2/14/2006	10.7 (5%)	—	—	—	—	0.030 (2%)	-10.7 ± 0.5	100	5	Y
10A to 12	10A, 11, 12	0.3	2/14/2006	0.030 (2%)	0 (0%)	—	—	—	0 (0%)	-0.030 ± 0.001	100	2	Y
12 to 13	12, 13	2.2	2/14/2006	0 (0%)	—	—	—	—	0 (0%)	0 ± 0	—	—	—
13 to 14	13, 14	2.2	2/14/2006	0 (0%)	—	—	—	—	0 (0%)	0 ± 0	—	—	—
14 to 16	14, 15, 16	4.6	2/14/2006	0 (0%)	0 (0%)	—	—	—	0 (0%)	0 ± 0	—	—	—
16 to 17	16, 17	4.9	2/14/2006	0 (0%)	—	—	—	—	0.090 (2%)	0.090 ± 0.002	100	2	Y
17 to 19	17, 18, 18A, 19	4.0	2/14/2006	0.090 (2%)	5.32 (5%)	0.37 (10%)	—	—	5.77 (5%)	-0.01 ± 0.39	0	7	N
19 to 21	19, 20, 21	2.3	2/14/2006	5.77 (5%)	4.05 (8%)	—	—	—	12.0 (5%)	2.2 ± 0.7	18	6	Y
21 to 22	21, 22	3.0	2/14/2006	12.0 (5%)	—	—	—	—	12.3 (5%)	0.3 ± 0.9	3	7	N
22 to 25	22, 23, 24, 25	3.8	2/15/2006	11.5 (5%)	0.004 (2%)	2.28 (8%)	—	—	12.6 (5%)	-1.2 ± 0.9	9	6	Y
25 to 26	25, 25C, 26	3.1	2/15/2006	12.6 (5%)	2.2 (10%)	—	—	—	8.66 (5%)	-6.1 ± 0.8	42	5	Y
26 to 27	26, 27	2.3	2/15/2006	8.66 (5%)	—	—	—	—	6.14 (5%)	-2.52 ± 0.53	29	6	Y
27 to 28	27, 28	3.1	2/15/2006	6.14 (5%)	—	—	—	—	3.40 (8%)	-2.74 ± 0.41	45	7	Y
28 to 29	28, 29	3.4	2/15/2006	3.40 (8%)	—	—	—	—	2.41 (5%)	-0.99 ± 0.30	29	9	Y
29 to 31	29, 30, 31	1.9	2/15/2006	2.41 (5%)	2.54 (8%)	—	—	—	4.59 (5%)	-0.36 ± 0.33	7	7	Y
31 to 34	31, 32, 32A, 33, 33A, 34	1.0	2/15/2006	4.59 (5%)	16.3 (5%)	0.57 (10%)	0.076 (2%)	0.025 (2%)	22.0 (5%)	0.4 ± 1.4	2	6	N

[1]Subreach is defined as the interval between two adjacent river discharge-measurement locations.

A computed gain or loss for a subreach was considered meaningful if the percentage of normalized seepage difference (N_d) was greater than or equal to the percentage of normalized cumulative uncertainty (N_e). For example, in the 2006 seepage investigation (table 2), the estimated seepage loss (Q_S) for subreach "8 to 10" is -8.0 ± 1.6 ft³/s. This loss, as a percentage of the normalized seepage difference (N_d), is 43 percent of the maximum discharge (sum of upstream discharge and inflow) and is greater than the percentage of normalized cumulative uncertainty (N_e) of 8 percent, indicating that the loss is meaningful.

Seepage Investigations of the Rio Grande from Below Leasburg Dam, Leasburg, New Mexico, to Above American Dam, El Paso, Texas, from 2006 to 2013

2006 Seepage Investigation

The 2006 seepage investigation (February 14–15) focused on a 62.4-mile reach of the Rio Grande and included 39 measurement locations from site 1 in Leasburg, N. Mex., to site 34 in El Paso, Tex. (fig. 1, table 1). Sites 1 through 22 were measured on February 14, and sites 22 through 34 were measured on February 15. There was measurable discharge at 31 of the 39 measurement locations (19 river sites and 12 inflow sites; table 2); specific conductance and water temperature were also measured (app. 1). No measureable discharge occurred at 4 river and 4 inflow sites; the river was dry for at least 9 miles from downstream of site 10A to upstream of site 17. The median uncertainty in discharge measurements over the study reach was 5 percent. Precipitation of 0.05 inches was recorded at El Paso International Airport during the week prior to the seepage investigation (National Climatic Data Center, 2012), but no precipitation was recorded during the seepage investigation, and precipitation was assumed not to affect streamflow during the seepage investigation. Analysis of discharge measurements collected at site 22 on February 14 (12.3 ± 0.6 ft³/s) and on February 15 (11.5 ± 0.6 ft³/s) indicates that a decrease in streamflow of 0.8 ± 0.8 ft³/s occurred at this site during the 2-day seepage investigation. Although the variability in streamflow measured at site 22 during the seepage investigation may increase the uncertainty of the cumulative seepage gain or loss in streamflow computed over the entire study reach, it likely does not affect the estimation of net seepage gain or loss computed for individual subreaches.

Net seepage gain to or loss from the river and the associated cumulative uncertainty were computed for the 19 subreaches with measurable flow (table 2). The computed net seepage was less than the cumulative uncertainty at 4 of the 19 subreaches, indicating that the estimated gain or loss cannot be considered meaningful within those subreaches. Analysis of the sum of gains and losses computed for each subreach indicates a cumulative loss of 36.2 ± 2.7 ft³/s within the study reach (table 3).

2007 Seepage Investigation

The 2007 seepage investigation (February 13–14) focused on a 62.4-mile reach of the Rio Grande and included 37 measurement locations from site 1 in Leasburg, N. Mex., to site 34 in El Paso, Tex. (fig. 1, table 1). Sites 1 through 17 were measured on February 13, and sites 17 through 34 were measured on February 14. There was measurable discharge at 34 of the 37 measurement locations (22 river sites and 12 inflow sites; table 4); specific conductance and water temperature were also measured (app. 1). No measurable discharge occurred at three inflow sites. The median uncertainty in discharge measurements over the study reach was 5 percent. Isolated rain showers occurred during the seepage investigation, with 0.12 inches of precipitation recorded on February 13 and 0.04 inches of precipitation recorded on February 14 at El Paso International Airport (National Climatic Data Center, 2012); however, precipitation was assumed not to affect streamflow during the seepage investigation. Analysis of discharge measured at site 17 on February 13 (13.9 ± 0.7 ft³/s) and on February 14 (13.4 ± 0.7 ft³/s) indicates that streamflow decreased 0.5 ± 1.0 ft³/s at this site during the seepage investigation. Although the variability in streamflow measured at site 17 during the seepage investigation may increase the uncertainty of the cumulative seepage gain or loss in streamflow computed over the entire study reach, it likely does not affect the estimation of net seepage gain or loss computed for individual subreaches.

Table 3. Summary of the cumulative gain or loss in streamflow due to seepage along subreaches within the study reach, Rio Grande seepage investigations, 2006–13.

[Q_S, net seepage gain or loss. See text for equations and description of uncertainty computation; ft³/s, cubic foot per second; -, minus; ±, plus or minus]

Year	Length of study reach (miles)	Cumulative sum of Q_S (ft³/s)
2006	62.4	-36.2 ± 2.7
2007	62.4	-36.3 ± 6.7
2008	62.4	-41.4 ± 3.5
2009	62.4	-47.9 ± 8.2
2010	20.2	-10.5 ± 3.4
2011	20.2	-8.2 ± 3.1
2012	64	-16.2 ± 2.1
2013	64	-19.3 ± 2.5

Table 4. Summary of measured discharge and the computed net seepage gain or loss in streamflow along river subreaches, Rio Grande seepage investigation, February 13–14, 2007.

[Site number: see table 1 and figures 1 and 2 for locations of sites; Q_{us}, discharge measured at upstream river channel site; ft³/s, cubic foot per second; ±, plus or minus; Q_{in}, discharge measured at inflow site (individual subreaches had between 0 and 4 inflows; subscript number indicates inflow site 1, 2, 3, or 4, ordered upstream to downstream); Q_{ds}, discharge measured at downstream river channel site; Q_s, net seepage gain or loss. See text for equations, description of cumulative uncertainty computation, and definitions of terms; $N_d\%$, normalized percentage difference, used to determine the difference between discharge measured at upstream and downstream sites of a given subreach. $N_e\%$, normalized percentage error, used to determine if a computed gain or loss exceeds errors associated with discharge measurement. ≥, greater than or equal to; Y, yes; N, no; %, percent; —, not applicable]

Subreach[1]	Sites included in subreach[1]	Distance (miles)	Sample date	Q_{us} with percentage of measurement uncertainty in parentheses (ft³/s)	Q_{in1} with percentage of measurement uncertainty in parentheses (ft³/s)	Q_{in2} with percentage of measurement uncertainty in parentheses (ft³/s)	Q_{in3} with percentage of measurement uncertainty in parentheses (ft³/s)	Q_{in4} with percentage of measurement uncertainty in parentheses (ft³/s)	Q_{ds} with percentage of measurement uncertainty in parentheses (ft³/s)	Q_s (ft³/s)	Normalized percentage difference ($N_d\%$)	Normalized percentage error ($N_e\%$)	$N_d\% \geq N_e\%$ (Y or N)
1 to 2	1, 2	2.1	2/13/2007	28.7 (8%)	—	—	—	—	31.0 (5%)	2.3 ± 2.8	7	9	N
2 to 4	2, 3, 4	3.9	2/13/2007	31.0 (5%)	0 (0%)	—	—	—	31.8 (5%)	0.8 ± 2.2	3	7	N
4 to 5	4, 5	3.6	2/13/2007	31.8 (5%)	—	—	—	—	33.4 (5%)	1.6 ± 2.3	5	7	N
5 to 7	5, 6, 7	3.9	2/13/2007	33.4 (5%)	0 (0%)	—	—	—	18.2 (5%)	−15.2 ± 1.9	46	6	Y
7 to 8	7, 8	3.2	2/13/2007	18.2 (5%)	—	—	—	—	20.9 (8%)	2.7 ± 1.9	13	9	Y
8 to 10	8, 9, 10	2.5	2/13/2007	20.9 (8%)	12.9 (8%)	—	—	—	33.5 (8%)	−0.3 ± 3.3	1	10	N
10 to 12	10, 11, 12	1.1	2/13/2007	33.5 (8%)	0.069 (2%)	—	—	—	30.3 (5%)	−3.3 ± 3.1	10	9	Y
12 to 13	12, 13	2.2	2/13/2007	30.3 (5%)	—	—	—	—	18.3 (5%)	−12.0 ± 1.8	40	6	Y
13 to 14	13, 14	2.2	2/13/2007	18.3 (5%)	—	—	—	—	18.1 (5%)	−0.2 ± 1.3	1	7	N
14 to 16	14, 15, 16	4.6	2/13/2007	18.1 (5%)	0 (0%)	—	—	—	15.0 (5%)	−3.1 ± 1.2	17	6	Y
16 to 17	16, 17	4.9	2/13/2007	15.0 (5%)	—	—	—	—	13.9 (5%)	−1.1 ± 1.0	7	7	Y
17 to 19	17, 18, 18A, 19	4.0	2/14/2007	13.4 (5%)	4.86 (5%)	0.39 (10%)	—	—	16.3 (5%)	−2.4 ± 1.1	13	6	Y
19 to 21	19, 20, 21	2.3	2/14/2007	16.3 (5%)	0.001 (2%)	—	—	—	17.1 (8%)	0.8 ± 1.6	5	9	N
21 to 22	21, 22	3.0	2/14/2007	17.1 (8%)	—	—	—	—	18.8 (5%)	1.7 ± 1.7	9	9	Y
22 to 25	22, 23, 24, 25	3.8	2/14/2007	18.8 (5%)	0.010 (5%)	3.31 (8%)	—	—	24.7 (5%)	2.6 ± 1.6	10	6	Y
25 to 26	25, 26	3.1	2/14/2007	24.7 (5%)	—	—	—	—	21.4 (5%)	−3.3 ± 1.6	13	7	Y
26 to 27	26, 27	2.3	2/14/2007	21.4 (5%)	—	—	—	—	19.3 (5%)	−2.1 ± 1.4	10	7	Y
27 to 28	27, 28	3.1	2/14/2007	19.3 (5%)	—	—	—	—	15.6 (5%)	−3.7 ± 1.2	19	6	Y
28 to 29	28, 29	3.4	2/14/2007	15.6 (5%)	—	—	—	—	12.0 (5%)	−3.6 ± 1.0	23	6	Y
29 to 31	29, 30, 31	1.9	2/14/2007	12.0 (5%)	3.01 (8%)	—	—	—	14.5 (8%)	−0.5 ± 1.3	3	9	N
31 to 34	31, 32, 32A, 33, 33A, 34	1.0	2/14/2007	14.5 (8%)	20.8 (5%)	0.60 (10%)	0.565 (10%)	0.013 (2%)	38.4 (5%)	1.9 ± 2.5	5	6	N

[1]Subreach is defined as the interval between two adjacent river discharge-measurement locations.

Net seepage gain to or loss from the river and the associated cumulative uncertainty were computed for all 21 subreaches (table 4). The computed net seepage was less than the cumulative uncertainty at 8 of the 21 subreaches, indicating that the estimated gain or loss cannot be considered meaningful within those subreaches. Analysis of the sum of gains and losses computed for each subreach indicates a cumulative loss of 36.3 ± 6.7 ft³/s within the study reach (table 3).

2008 Seepage Investigation

The 2008 seepage investigation (February 12–13) focused on a 62.4-mile reach of the Rio Grande and included 37 measurement locations from site 1 in Leasburg, N. Mex., to site 34 in El Paso, Tex. (fig. 1, table 1). Sites 1 through 17 were measured on February 12, and sites 17 through 34 were measured on February 13. There was measurable discharge at 33 of the 37 measurement locations (22 river sites and 11 inflow sites; table 5); specific conductance and water temperature were also measured (app. 1). No measurable discharge occurred at four inflow sites. The median uncertainty in discharge measurements over the study reach was 5 percent. No precipitation occurred at El Paso International Airport during or for the week prior to the seepage investigation (National Climatic Data Center, 2012). Analysis of discharge measured at site 17 on February 12 (0.200 ± 0.020 ft³/s) and on February 13 (0.736 ± 0.074 ft³/s) indicates an increase in streamflow of 0.536 ± 0.077 ft³/s at this site during the seepage investigation. Although the variability in streamflow measured at site 17 during the seepage investigation may increase the uncertainty of the cumulative seepage gain or loss in streamflow computed over the entire study reach, it likely does not affect the estimation of net seepage gain or loss computed for individual subreaches.

Net seepage gain to or loss from the river and the associated cumulative uncertainty were computed for all 21 subreaches (table 5). The computed net seepage was less than the cumulative uncertainty at 2 of the 21 subreaches, indicating that the estimated gain or loss cannot be considered meaningful within those subreaches. Analysis of the sum of gains and losses computed for each subreach indicates a cumulative loss of 41.4 ± 3.5 ft³/s within the study reach (table 3).

2009 Seepage Investigation

The 2009 seepage investigation (February 10–11) focused on a 62.4-mile reach of the Rio Grande and included 38 measurement locations from site 1 in Leasburg, N. Mex., to site 34 in El Paso, Tex. (fig. 1, table 1). Sites 1 through 17 were measured on February 10, and sites 17 through 34 were measured on February 11. There was measurable discharge at 33 of the 38 measurement locations (22 river sites and 11 inflow sites; table 6); specific conductance and water temperature were also measured (app. 1). No measurable discharge occurred at five inflow sites. The median uncertainty in discharge measurements over the study reach was 5 percent. No precipitation occurred at El Paso International Airport during or for the week prior to the seepage investigation (National Climatic Data Center, 2012). Analysis of discharge measured at site 17 on February 10 (18.0 ± 0.9 ft³/s) and on February 11 (15.3 ± 1.2 ft³/s) indicates that streamflow decreased 2.7 ± 1.5 ft³/s at this site during the seepage investigation. Although the variability in streamflow measured at site 17 during the seepage investigation may increase the uncertainty of the cumulative seepage gain or loss in streamflow computed over the entire study reach, it likely does not affect the estimation of net seepage gain or loss computed for individual subreaches.

Net seepage gain to or loss from the river and the associated cumulative uncertainty were computed for all 21 subreaches (table 6). The computed net seepage was less than the cumulative uncertainty at 6 of the 21 subreaches, indicating that the estimated gain or loss cannot be considered significant within those subreaches. Analysis of the sum of gains and losses computed for each subreach indicates a cumulative loss of 47.9 ± 8.2 ft³/s within the study reach (table 3).

2010 Seepage Investigation

The 2010 seepage investigation (February 23) focused on a 20.2-mile reach of the Rio Grande and included 19 measurement locations from site 22 in Anthony, N. Mex., to site 36 in El Paso, Tex. (fig. 1, table 1). There was measurable discharge at 18 of the 19 measurement locations (9 river sites and 9 inflow sites; table 7); specific conductance and water temperature were also measured (app. 1). No measurable discharge occurred at one inflow site. The median uncertainty in discharge measurements over the study reach was 5 percent. Precipitation of 0.07 inches was recorded at El Paso International Airport during the week prior to the seepage investigation (National Climatic Data Center, 2012), but no precipitation was recorded during the seepage investigation, and precipitation was assumed not to affect streamflow during the seepage investigation.

Net seepage gain to or loss from the river and the associated cumulative uncertainty were computed for all eight subreaches (table 7). The computed net seepage was less than the cumulative uncertainty at 1 of the 8 subreaches, indicating that the estimated gain or loss cannot be considered meaningful within that subreach. Analysis of the sum of gains and losses computed for each subreach indicates a cumulative loss of 10.5 ± 3.4 ft³/s within the study reach (table 3).

Table 5. Summary of measured discharge and the computed net seepage gain or loss in streamflow along river subreaches, Rio Grande seepage investigation, February 12–13, 2008.

[Site number: see table 1 and figures 1 and 2 for locations of sites; Q_{us}, discharge measured at upstream river channel site; ft³/s, cubic foot per second; ±, plus or minus; Q_{in}, discharge measured at inflow site (individual subreaches had between 0 and 4 inflows; subscript number indicates inflow site 1, 2, 3, or 4, ordered upstream to downstream); Q_{ds}, discharge measured at downstream river channel site; Q_s, net seepage gain or loss. See text for equations, description of cumulative uncertainty computation, and definitions of terms; $N_d\%$, normalized percentage difference, used to determine the difference between discharge measured at upstream and downstream sites of a given subreach. $N_e\%$, normalized percentage error, used to determine if a computed gain or loss exceeds errors associated with discharge measurement. ≥, greater than or equal to; Y, yes; N, no; %, percent; —, not applicable]

Sub-reach[1]	Sites included in subreach[1]	Distance (miles)	Sample date	Q_{us} with percentage of measurement uncertainty in parentheses (ft³/s)	Q_{in1} with percentage of measurement uncertainty in parentheses (ft³/s)	Q_{in2} with percentage of measurement uncertainty in parentheses (ft³/s)	Q_{in3} with percentage of measurement uncertainty in parentheses (ft³/s)	Q_{in4} with percentage of measurement uncertainty in parentheses (ft³/s)	Q_{ds} with percentage of measurement uncertainty in parentheses (ft³/s)	Q_s (ft³/s)	Normalized percentage difference ($N_d\%$)	Normalized percentage error ($N_e\%$)	$N_d\% \geq N_e\%$ (Y or N)
1 to 2	1, 2	2.1	2/12/2008	17.7 (5%)	—	—	—	—	19.3 (5%)	1.6 ± 1.3	8	7	Y
2 to 4	2, 3, 4	3.9	2/12/2008	19.3 (5%)	0 (0%)	—	—	—	21.3 (5%)	2.0 ± 1.4	9	7	Y
4 to 5	4, 5	3.6	2/12/2008	21.3 (5%)	—	—	—	—	19.1 (5%)	-2.2 ± 1.4	10	7	Y
5 to 7	5, 6, 7	3.9	2/12/2008	19.1 (5%)	0 (0%)	—	—	—	15.8 (5%)	-3.3 ± 1.2	17	6	Y
7 to 8	7, 8	3.2	2/12/2008	15.8 (5%)	—	—	—	—	9.82 (5%)	-6.0 ± 0.9	38	6	Y
8 to 10	8, 9, 10	2.5	2/12/2008	9.82 (5%)	17.0 (8%)	—	—	—	19.4 (5%)	-7.4 ± 1.7	28	6	Y
10 to 12	10, 11, 12	1.1	2/12/2008	19.4 (5%)	0 (0%)	—	—	—	13.6 (5%)	-5.8 ± 1.2	30	6	Y
12 to 13	12, 13	2.2	2/12/2008	13.6 (5%)	—	—	—	—	6.10 (8%)	-7.5 ± 0.8	55	6	Y
13 to 14	13, 14	2.2	2/12/2008	6.10 (8%)	—	—	—	—	6.89 (8%)	0.79 ± 0.74	11	11	Y
14 to 16	14, 15, 16	4.6	2/12/2008	6.89 (8%)	0 (0%)	—	—	—	2.24 (5%)	-4.65 ± 0.56	67	8	Y
16 to 17	16, 17	4.9	2/12/2008	2.24 (5%)	—	—	—	—	0.200 (10%)	-2.04 ± 0.11	91	5	Y
17 to 19	17, 18, 18A, 19	4.0	2/13/2008	0.736 (10%)	4.79 (5%)	0.43 (10%)	—	—	5.75 (5%)	-0.21 ± 0.38	3	6	N
19 to 21	19, 20, 21	2.3	2/13/2008	5.75 (5%)	2.43 (5%)	—	—	—	10.2 (5%)	2.02 ± 0.60	20	6	Y
21 to 22	21, 22	3.0	2/13/2008	10.2 (5%)	—	—	—	—	10.4 (5%)	0.2 ± 0.7	2	7	N
22 to 25	22, 23, 24, 25	3.8	2/13/2008	10.4 (5%)	0.090 (8%)	2.85 (5%)	—	—	12.0 (5%)	-1.3 ± 0.8	10	6	Y
25 to 26	25, 26	3.1	2/13/2008	12.0 (5%)	—	—	—	—	9.77 (5%)	-2.2 ± 0.8	19	6	Y
26 to 27	26, 27	2.3	2/13/2008	9.77 (5%)	—	—	—	—	7.31 (5%)	-2.46 ± 0.61	25	6	Y
27 to 28	27, 28	3.1	2/13/2008	7.31 (5%)	—	—	—	—	3.90 (5%)	-3.41 ± 0.41	47	6	Y
28 to 29	28, 29	3.4	2/13/2008	3.90 (5%)	—	—	—	—	0.892 (5%)	-3.01 ± 0.20	77	5	Y
29 to 31	29, 30, 31	1.9	2/13/2008	0.892 (5%)	2.77 (8%)	—	—	—	2.60 (5%)	-1.06 ± 0.26	29	7	Y
31 to 34	31, 32, 32A, 33, 33A, 34	1.0	2/13/2008	2.60 (5%)	15.8 (5%)	0.13 (10%)	0.286 (10%)	0.057 (5%)	23.5 (5%)	4.6 ± 1.4	20	6	Y

[1]Subreach is defined as the interval between two adjacent river discharge-measurement locations.

Table 6. Summary of measured discharge and the computed net seepage gain or loss in streamflow along river subreaches, Rio Grande seepage investigation, February 10–11, 2009.

[Site number: see table 1 and figures 1 and 2 for locations of sites; Q_{us}, discharge measured at upstream river channel site; Q_{in}, discharge measured at inflow site (individual subreaches had between 0 and 4 inflows; subscript number indicates inflow site 1, 2, 3, or 4, ordered upstream to downstream); Q_{ds}, discharge measured at downstream river channel site; Q_s, net seepage gain or loss. See text for equations, description of cumulative uncertainty computation, and definitions of terms; $N_d\%$, normalized percentage difference, used to determine the difference between discharge measured at upstream and downstream sites of a given subreach. $N_e\%$, normalized percentage error, used to determine if a computed gain or loss exceeds errors associated with discharge measurement. ≥, greater than or equal to; Y, yes; N, no; %, percent; —, not applicable]

Sub-reach[1]	Sites included in subreach[1]	Distance (miles)	Sample date	Q_{us} with percentage of measurement uncertainty in parentheses (ft³/s)	Q_{in1} with percentage of measurement uncertainty in parentheses (ft³/s)	Q_{in2} with percentage of measurement uncertainty in parentheses (ft³/s)	Q_{in3} with percentage of measurement uncertainty in parentheses (ft³/s)	Q_{in4} with percentage of measurement uncertainty in parentheses (ft³/s)	Q_{ds} with percentage of measurement uncertainty in parentheses (ft³/s)	Q_s (ft³/s)	Normalized percentage difference (N_d %)	Normalized percentage error (N_e %)	$N_d\% \geq N_e\%$ (Y or N)
1 to 2	1, 2	2.1	2/10/2009	31.0 (5%)	—				34.5 (5%)	3.5 ± 2.3	10	7	Y
2 to 4	2, 3, 4	3.9	2/10/2009	34.5 (5%)	0 (0%)				38.2 (5%)	3.7 ± 2.6	10	7	Y
4 to 5	4, 5	3.6	2/10/2009	38.2 (5%)	—				34.2 (5%)	-4.0 ± 2.6	10	7	Y
5 to 7	5, 6, 7	3.9	2/10/2009	34.2 (5%)	0 (0%)				34.9 (5%)	0.7 ± 2.4	2	7	N
7 to 8	7, 8	3.2	2/10/2009	34.9 (5%)	17.5 (8%)				28.5 (5%)	-6.4 ± 2.3	18	6	Y
8 to 10	8, 9, 10	2.5	2/10/2009	28.5 (5%)	0 (0%)				39.4 (5%)	-6.6 ± 2.8	14	6	Y
10 to 12	10, 11, 12	1.1	2/10/2009	39.4 (5%)	0 (0%)				34.9 (5%)	-4.5 ± 2.6	11	7	Y
12 to 13	12, 13	2.2	2/10/2009	34.9 (5%)	—				25.6 (8%)	-9.3 ± 2.7	27	8	Y
13 to 14	13, 14	2.2	2/10/2009	25.6 (8%)	—				24.6 (8%)	-1.0 ± 2.8	4	11	N
14 to 16	14, 15, 16	4.6	2/10/2009	24.6 (8%)	0 (0%)				17.4 (8%)	-7.2 ± 2.4	29	10	Y
16 to 17	16, 17	4.9	2/10/2009	17.4 (8%)	—				18.0 (5%)	0.6 ± 1.7	3	9	N
17 to 19	17, 18, 18A, 19	4.0	2/11/2009	15.3 (8%)	4.16 (8%)	0.48 (10%)			17.9 (5%)	-2.0 ± 1.6	10	8	Y
19 to 21	19, 20, 21	2.3	2/11/2009	17.9 (5%)	4.50 (5%)				23.2 (5%)	0.8 ± 1.5	3	6	N
21 to 22	21, 21A, 22	3.0	2/11/2009	23.2 (5%)	1.13 (8%)				25.9 (8%)	1.6 ± 2.4	6	9	N
22 to 25	22, 23, 24, 25	3.8	2/11/2009	25.9 (8%)	0.025 (5%)	3.27 (10%)			30.8 (8%)	1.6 ± 3.2	5	11	N
25 to 26	25, 26	3.1	2/11/2009	30.8 (8%)	—				26.6 (8%)	-4.2 ± 3.3	14	11	Y
26 to 27	26, 27	2.3	2/11/2009	26.6 (8%)	—				23.5 (5%)	-3.1 ± 2.4	12	9	Y
27 to 28	27, 28	3.1	2/11/2009	23.5 (5%)	—				20.5 (5%)	-3.0 ± 1.6	13	7	Y
28 to 29	28, 29	3.4	2/11/2009	20.5 (5%)	—				14.1 (5%)	-6.4 ± 1.2	31	6	Y
29 to 31	29, 30, 31	1.9	2/11/2009	14.1 (5%)	2.42 (8%)				18.2 (5%)	1.7 ± 1.2	9	6	Y
31 to 34	31, 32, 32A, 33, 33A, 34	1.0	2/11/2009	18.2 (5%)	20.0 (5%)	0 (0%)	0.576 (10%)	0.025 (5%)	34.5 (8%)	-4.3 ± 3.1	11	8	Y

[1]Subreach is defined as the interval between two adjacent river discharge-measurement locations.

Table 7. Summary of measured discharge and the computed net seepage gain or loss in streamflow along river subreaches, Rio Grande seepage investigation, February 23, 2010.

[Site number: see table 1 and figures 1 and 2 for locations of sites; Q_{us}, discharge measured at upstream river channel site; ft³/s, cubic foot per second; ±, plus or minus; Q_{in}, discharge measured at inflow site (individual subreaches had between 0 and 4 inflows; subscript number indicates inflow site 1, 2, 3, or 4, ordered upstream to downstream); Q_{ds}, discharge measured at downstream river channel site; Q_s, net seepage gain or loss. See text for equations, description of cumulative uncertainty computation, and definitions of terms; $N_d\%$, normalized percentage difference, used to determine the difference between discharge measured at upstream and downstream sites of a given subreach. $N_e\%$, normalized percentage error, used to determine if a computed gain or loss exceeds errors associated with discharge measurement. ≥, greater than or equal to; Y, yes; N, no; %, percent; —, not applicable]

Sub-reach[1]	Sites included in subreach[1]	Distance (miles)	Sample date	Q_{us} with percentage of measurement uncertainty in parentheses (ft³/s)	Q_{in1} with percentage of measurement uncertainty in parentheses (ft³/s)	Q_{in2} with percentage of measurement uncertainty in parentheses (ft³/s)	Q_{in3} with percentage of measurement uncertainty in parentheses (ft³/s)	Q_{in4} with percentage of measurement uncertainty in parentheses (ft³/s)	Q_{ds} with percentage of measurement uncertainty in parentheses (ft³/s)	Q_s (ft³/s)	Normalized percentage difference ($N_d\%$)	Normalized percentage error ($N_e\%$)	$N_d\% \geq N_e\%$ (Y or N)
22 to 25	22, 23, 24, 25	3.8	2/23/2010	12.5 (8%)	0.021 (5%)	2.11 (8%)	—	—	12.6 (5%)	-2.0 ± 1.2	14	8	Y
25 to 26	25, 26	3.1	2/23/2010	12.6 (5%)	—	—	—	—	11.3 (5%)	-1.3 ± 0.8	10	7	Y
26 to 27	26, 27	2.3	2/23/2010	11.3 (5%)	—	—	—	—	9.80 (5%)	-1.5 ± 0.7	13	7	Y
27 to 28	27, 28	3.1	2/23/2010	9.80 (5%)	—	—	—	—	6.20 (5%)	-3.60 ± 0.60	37	6	Y
28 to 29	28, 29	3.4	2/23/2010	6.20 (5%)	—	—	—	—	3.60 (5%)	-2.60 ± 0.36	42	6	Y
29 to 31	29, 30, 31	1.9	2/23/2010	3.60 (5%)	2.11 (8%)	—	—	—	3.77 (5%)	-1.94 ± 0.31	34	5	Y
31 to 34	31, 32, 32A, 33, 33A, 34	1.0	2/23/2010	3.77 (5%)	19.5 (5%)	0 (0%)	0.729 (5%)	0.057 (5%)	27.7 (8%)	3.6 ± 2.4	13	9	Y
34 to 36	34, 34A, 34B, 35, 36	1.6	2/23/2010	27.7 (8%)	0.184 (2%)	1.40 (10%)	8.31 (8%)	—	36.4 (5%)	-1.2 ± 2.9	3	8	N

[1]Subreach is defined as the interval between two adjacent river discharge-measurement locations.

2011 Seepage Investigation

The 2011 seepage investigation (February 15) focused on a 20.2-mile reach of the Rio Grande and included 18 measurement locations from site 22 in Anthony, N. Mex., to site 36 in El Paso, Tex. (fig. 1, table 1). There was measurable discharge at 13 of the 18 measurement locations (5 river sites and 8 inflow sites; table 8); specific conductance and water temperature were also measured (app. 1). No measurable discharge occurred at four river sites and one inflow site; the river was dry for at least 9 miles downstream of site 25 to upstream of site 31. The median uncertainty in discharge measurements over the study reach was 5 percent. No precipitation occurred at El Paso International Airport during the seepage investigation (National Climatic Data Center, 2012).

Net seepage gain to or loss from the river and the associated cumulative uncertainty were computed for the five subreaches with measurable flow (table 8). The computed net seepage was less than the cumulative uncertainty at 1 of the 5 subreaches, indicating that the estimated gain or loss cannot be considered meaningful within that subreach. Analysis of the sum of gains and losses computed for each subreach indicates a cumulative loss of 8.2 ± 3.1 ft^3/s within the study reach (table 3).

2012 Seepage Investigation

The 2012 seepage investigation (February 28) focused on a 64.0-mile reach of the Rio Grande and included 41 measurement locations from site 1 in Leasburg, N. Mex., to site 36 in El Paso, Tex. (fig. 1, table 1). There was measurable discharge at 16 of the 41 measurement locations (6 river sites and 10 inflow sites; table 9); specific conductance and water temperature were also measured (app. 1). No measurable discharge occurred at 17 river sites and 8 inflow sites; the river was dry for at least 57 miles downstream of site 2 to upstream of site 31, except for short intervals (less than 3 miles) immediately downstream of inflow sites 9, 18A, 21A, 23, and 30. The median uncertainty in discharge measurements over the study reach was 8 percent. The uncertainty in discharge was generally greater than previous years because of shallow water depths and poor channel conditions. No precipitation occurred at El Paso International

Airport during the seepage investigation (National Climatic Data Center, 2012).

Net seepage gain to or loss from the river and the associated cumulative uncertainty were computed for the 10 subreaches with measurable flow (table 9). The computed net seepage was less than the cumulative uncertainty at 3 of the 10 subreaches, indicating that the estimated gain or loss cannot be considered meaningful within those subreaches. Analysis of the sum of gains and losses computed for each subreach indicates a cumulative loss of 16.2 ± 2.1 ft^3/s within the study reach (table 3).

2013 Seepage Investigation

The 2013 seepage investigation (February 26) focused on a 64.0-mile reach of the Rio Grande and included 41 measurement locations from site 1 in Leasburg, N. Mex., to site 36 in El Paso, Tex. (fig. 1, table 1). There was measurable discharge at 15 of the 41 measurement locations (6 river sites and 9 inflow sites; table 10); specific conductance and water temperature were also measured (app. 1). No measurable discharge occurred at 17 river and 9 inflow sites; the river was dry for at least 57 miles downstream of site 2 to upstream of site 31, except for short intervals (less than 3 miles) immediately downstream of inflow from sites 9, 18A, 21A, 23, and 30. The median uncertainty in discharge measurements over the study reach was 8 percent. The uncertainty in discharge was generally greater than previous years because of shallow water depths and poor channel conditions. Precipitation of 0.4 inches was recorded at El Paso International Airport the week prior to the seepage investigation (National Climatic Data Center, 2013), but no precipitation was recorded during the seepage investigation, and precipitation was assumed not to affect streamflow during the seepage investigation.

Net seepage gain to or loss from the river and the associated cumulative uncertainty were computed for the 10 subreaches with measurable flow (table 10). The computed net seepage was less than the cumulative uncertainty at 2 of the 10 subreaches, indicating that the estimated gain or loss cannot be considered meaningful within those subreaches. The sum of gains and losses computed for each subreach indicates a cumulative loss of 19.3 ± 2.5 ft^3/s within the study reach (table 3).

Table 8. Summary of measured discharge and the computed net seepage gain or loss in streamflow along river subreaches, Rio Grande seepage investigation, February 15, 2011.

[Site number: see table 1 and figures 1 and 2 for locations of sites; Q_{us}, discharge measured at upstream river channel site; ft³/s, cubic foot per second; ±, plus or minus; Q_m, discharge measured at inflow site (individual subreaches had between 0 and 4 inflows; subscript number indicates inflow site 1, 2, 3, or 4, ordered upstream to downstream); Q_{ds}, discharge measured at downstream river channel site; Q_s, net seepage gain or loss. See text for equations, description of cumulative uncertainty computation, and definitions of terms; $N_d\%$, normalized percentage difference, used to determine the difference between discharge measured at upstream and downstream sites of a given subreach. $N_e\%$, normalized percentage error, used to determine if a computed gain or loss exceeds errors associated with discharge measurement. ≥, greater than or equal to; Y, yes; N, no; %, percent; —, not applicable]

Sub-reach[1]	Sites included in subreach[1]	Dis-tance (miles)	Sample date	Q_{us} with percentage of measurement uncertainty in parentheses (ft³/s)	Q_{in1} with percentage of measurement uncertainty in parentheses (ft³/s)	Q_{in2} with percentage of measurement uncertainty in parentheses (ft³/s)	Q_{in3} with percentage of measurement uncertainty in parentheses (ft³/s)	Q_{in4} with percentage of measurement uncertainty in parentheses (ft³/s)	Q_{ds} with percentage of measurement uncertainty in parentheses (ft³/s)	Q_s (ft³/s)	Normalized percentage difference ($N_d\%$)	Normalized percentage error ($N_e\%$)	$N_d\% ≥ N_e\%$ (Y or N)
22 to 25	22, 23, 24, 25	3.8	2/15/2011	5.14 (8%)	0.013 (5%)	0.890 (8%)	—	—	3.41 (5%)	-2.63 ± 0.45	44	7	Y
25 to 26	25, 26	3.1	2/15/2011	3.41 (5%)	—	—	—	—	0 (0%)	-3.41 ± 0.17	100	5	Y
26 to 27	26, 27	2.3	2/15/2011	0 (0%)	—	—	—	—	0 (0%)	0 ± 0	—	—	—
27 to 28	27, 28	3.1	2/15/2011	0 (0%)	—	—	—	—	0 (0%)	0 ± 0	—	—	—
28 to 29	28, 29	3.4	2/15/2011	0 (0%)	—	—	—	—	0 (0%)	0 ± 0	—	—	—
29 to 31	29, 30, 31	1.9	2/15/2011	0 (0%)	2.2 (8%)	—	—	—	3.26 (8%)	1.05 ± 0.32	32	10	Y
31 to 34	31, 32, 32A, 33, 33A, 34	1.0	2/15/2011	3.26 (8%)	15.6 (5%)	0 (0%)	0.533 (8%)	0.045 (2%)	17.6 (5%)	-1.8 ± 1.2	9	6	Y
34 to 36	34, 34A, 35, 36	1.6	2/15/2011	17.6 (5%)	0.135 (5%)	24.8 (8%)	—	—	41.2 (5%)	-1.3 ± 3.0	3	7	N

[1]Subreach is defined as the interval between two adjacent river discharge-measurement locations.

Table 9. Summary of measured discharge and the computed net seepage gain or loss in streamflow along river subreaches, Rio Grande seepage investigation, February 28, 2012.

[Site number: see table 1 and figures 1 and 2 for locations of sites; Q_{us}, discharge measured at upstream river channel site; ft³/s, cubic foot per second; ±, plus or minus; Q_{in}, discharge measured at inflow site (individual subreaches had between 0 and 4 inflows; subscript number indicates inflow site 1, 2, 3, or 4, ordered upstream to downstream); Q_{ds}, discharge measured at downstream river channel site; Q_s, net seepage gain or loss. See text for equations, description of cumulative uncertainty computation, and definitions of terms; N_d%, normalized percentage difference, used to determine the difference between discharge measured at upstream and downstream sites of a given subreach. N_e%, normalized percentage error, used to determine if a computed gain or loss exceeds errors associated with discharge measurement. ≥, greater than or equal to; Y, yes; N, no; %, percent; —, not applicable]

Sub-reach[1]	Sites included in subreach[1]	Distance (miles)	Sample date	Q_{us} with percentage of measurement uncertainty in parentheses (ft³/s)	Q_{in1} with percentage of measurement uncertainty in parentheses (ft³/s)	Q_{in2} with percentage of measurement uncertainty in parentheses (ft³/s)	Q_{in3} with percentage of measurement uncertainty in parentheses (ft³/s)	Q_{in4} with percentage of measurement uncertainty in parentheses (ft³/s)	Q_{ds} with percentage of measurement uncertainty in parentheses (ft³/s)	Q_s (ft³/s)	Normalized percentage difference (N_d%)	Normalized percentage error (N_e%)	N_d% ≥ N_e% (Y or N)
1 to 2	1, 2	2.1	2/28/2012	1.31 (8%)	—				0.866 (8%)	-0.44 ± 0.13	34	10	Y
2 to 4	2, 3, 4	3.9	2/28/2012	0.866 (8%)	0 (0%)				0 (0%)	-0.866 ± 0.069	100	8	Y
4 to 5	4, 5	3.6	2/28/2012	0 (0%)	—				0 (0%)	0 ± 0	—	—	—
5 to 7	5, 6, 7	3.9	2/28/2012	0 (0%)	0 (0%)				0 (0%)	0 ± 0	—	—	—
7 to 8	7, 8	3.2	2/28/2012	0 (0%)	—				0 (0%)	0 ± 0	—	—	—
8 to 10	8, 9, 10	2.5	2/28/2012	0 (0%)	12.7 (8%)				4.37 (8%)	-8.3 ± 1.1	66	8	Y
10 to 12	10, 11, 12	1.1	2/28/2012	4.37 (8%)	0 (0%)				0 (0%)	-4.37 ± 0.35	100	8	Y
12 to 13	12, 13	2.2	2/28/2012	0 (0%)	—				0 (0%)	0 ± 0	—	—	—
13 to 14	13, 14	2.2	2/28/2012	0 (0%)	0 (0%)				0 (0%)	0 ± 0	—	—	—
14 to 16	14, 15, 16	4.6	2/28/2012	0 (0%)	0 (0%)				0 (0%)	0 ± 0	—	—	—
16 to 17	16, 17	4.9	2/28/2012	0 (0%)	—				0 (0%)	0 ± 0	—	—	—
17 to 19	17, 18, 18A, 19	4.0	2/28/2012	0 (0%)	0 (0%)	0.54 (10%)			0 (0%)	-0.540 ± 0.054	100	10	Y
19 to 21	19, 20, 21	2.3	2/28/2012	0 (0%)	0 (0%)				0 (0%)	0 ± 0	—	—	—
21 to 22	21, 21A, 22	3.0	2/28/2012	0 (0%)	0.535 (8%)				0 (0%)	-0.535 ± 0.043	100	8	Y
22 to 25	22, 23, 24, 25	3.8	2/28/2012	0 (0%)	0.090 (8%)	0 (0%)			0 (0%)	-0.090 ± 0.007	100	8	Y
25 to 26	25, 26	3.1	2/28/2012	0 (0%)	—				0 (0%)	0 ± 0	—	—	—
26 to 27	26, 27	2.3	2/28/2012	0 (0%)	—				0 (0%)	0 ± 0	—	—	—
27 to 28	27, 28	3.1	2/28/2012	0 (0%)	—				0 (0%)	0 ± 0	—	—	—
28 to 29	28, 29	3.4	2/28/2012	0 (0%)	—				0 (0%)	0 ± 0	—	—	—
29 to 31	29, 30, 31	1.9	2/28/2012	2.06 (8%)	2.14 (8%)				2.06 (8%)	-0.08 ± 0.24	4	12	N
31 to 34	31, 32, 32A, 33, 33A, 34	1.0	2/28/2012	2.06 (8%)	5.89 (5%)	0 (0%)	0.412 (10%)	0.030 (2%)	8.12 (5%)	-0.27 ± 0.53	3	6	N
34 to 36	34, 34A, 35, 36	1.6	2/28/2012	8.12 (5%)	0.104 (2%)	15.3 (8%)			22.9 (5%)	-0.6 ± 1.7	3	7	N

[1]Subreach is defined as the interval between two adjacent river discharge-measurement locations.

Table 10. Summary of measured discharge and the computed net seepage gain or loss in streamflow along river subreaches, Rio Grande seepage investigation, February 26, 2013.

[Site number: see table 1 and figures 1 and 2 for locations of sites; Q_{us}, discharge measured at upstream river channel site; ft³/s, cubic foot per second; ±, plus or minus; Q_{in}, discharge measured at inflow site (individual subreaches had between 0 and 4 inflows; subscript number indicates inflow site 1, 2, 3, or 4, ordered upstream to downstream); Q_{ds}, discharge measured at downstream river channel site; Q_s, net seepage gain or loss. See text for equations, description of cumulative uncertainty computation, and definitions of terms; Nd%, normalized percentage difference, used to determine the difference between discharge measured at upstream and downstream sites of a given subreach. Ne%, normalized percentage error, used to determine if a computed gain or loss exceeds errors associated with discharge measurement. ≥, greater than or equal to; Y, yes; N, no; %, percent; ——, not applicable]

Subreach[1]	Sites included in subreach[1]	Distance (miles)	Sample date	Q_{us} with percentage of measurement uncertainty in parentheses (ft³/s)	Q_{in1} with percentage of measurement uncertainty in parentheses (ft³/s)	Q_{in2} with percentage of measurement uncertainty in parentheses (ft³/s)	Q_{in3} with percentage of measurement uncertainty in parentheses (ft³/s)	Q_{in4} with percentage of measurement uncertainty in parentheses (ft³/s)	Q_{ds} with percentage of measurement uncertainty in parentheses (ft³/s)	Q_s (ft³/s)	Normalized percentage difference (N$_d$%)	Normalized percentage error (N$_e$%)	N$_d$% ≥ N$_e$% (Y or N)
1 to 2	1, 2	2.1	2/26/2013	0.696 (10%)	——	——	——	——	0.353 (10%)	−0.343 ± 0.078	49	11	Y
2 to 4	2, 3, 4	3.9	2/26/2013	0.353 (10%)	0 (0%)	——	——	——	0 (0%)	−0.353 ± 0.035	100	10	Y
4 to 5	4, 5	3.6	2/26/2013	0 (0%)	0 (0%)	——	——	——	0 (0%)	0 ± 0	——	——	——
5 to 7	5, 6, 7	3.9	2/26/2013	0 (0%)	0 (0%)	——	——	——	0 (0%)	0 ± 0	——	——	——
7 to 8	7, 8	3.2	2/26/2013	0 (0%)	——	——	——	——	0 (0%)	0 ± 0	——	——	——
8 to 10	8, 9, 10	2.5	2/26/2013	0 (0%)	15.8 (8%)	——	——	——	2.77 (10%)	−13.0 ± 1.3	82	8	Y
10 to 12	10, 11, 12	1.1	2/26/2013	2.77 (10%)	0 (0%)	——	——	——	0 (0%)	−2.77 ± 0.28	100	10	Y
12 to 13	12, 13	2.2	2/26/2013	0 (0%)	0 (0%)	——	——	——	0 (0%)	0 ± 0	——	——	——
13 to 14	13, 14	2.2	2/26/2013	0 (0%)	——	——	——	——	0 (0%)	0 ± 0	——	——	——
14 to 16	14, 15, 16	4.6	2/26/2013	0 (0%)	0 (0%)	——	——	——	0 (0%)	0 ± 0	——	——	——
16 to 17	16, 17	4.9	2/26/2013	0 (0%)	——	——	——	——	0 (0%)	0 ± 0	——	——	——
17 to 19	17, 18, 18A, 19	4.0	2/26/2013	0 (0%)	0 (0%)	0.48 (10%)	——	——	0 (0%)	−0.480 ± 0.048	100	10	Y
19 to 21	19, 20, 21	2.3	2/26/2013	0 (0%)	0 (0%)	——	——	——	0 (0%)	0 ± 0	——	——	——
21 to 22	21, 21A, 22	3.0	2/26/2013	0 (0%)	0.668 (8%)	——	——	——	0 (0%)	−0.668 ± 0.053	100	8	Y
22 to 25	22, 23, 24, 25	3.8	2/26/2013	0 (0%)	0.025 (5%)	0 (0%)	——	——	0 (0%)	−0.025 ± 0.001	100	5	Y
25 to 26	25, 26	3.1	2/26/2013	0 (0%)	——	——	——	——	0 (0%)	0 ± 0	——	——	——
26 to 27	26, 27	2.3	2/26/2013	0 (0%)	——	——	——	——	0 (0%)	0 ± 0	——	——	——
27 to 28	27, 28	3.1	2/26/2013	0 (0%)	——	——	——	——	0 (0%)	0 ± 0	——	——	——
28 to 29	28, 29	3.4	2/26/2013	0 (0%)	——	——	——	——	0 (0%)	0 ± 0	——	——	——
29 to 31	29, 30, 31	1.9	2/26/2013	0 (0%)	2.77 (8%)	——	——	——	2.42 (5%)	−0.35 ± 0.25	14	10	Y
31 to 34	31, 32, 32A, 33, 33A, 34	1.0	2/26/2013	2.42 (8%)	5.61 (10%)	0 (0%)	0.358 (8%)	0 (0%)	8.64 (5%)	0.25 ± 0.74	3	9	N
34 to 36	34, 34A, 35, 36	1.6	2/26/2013	8.64 (5%)	0.170 (8%)	11.2 (8%)	——	——	18.5 (10%)	−1.5 ± 2.1	8	10	N

[1]Subreach is defined as the interval between two adjacent river discharge-measurement locations.

Summary

Increasing water demand within the Mesilla Basin and adjacent areas has resulted in increased groundwater withdrawals in the basin. In 1987, the U.S. Geological Survey (USGS) established the Mesilla Basin monitoring program to document and identify trends in groundwater conditions and stream/aquifer relations. Seepage investigations along a 64-mile reach of the Rio Grande from below Leasburg Dam, New Mexico, to above American Dam, El Paso, Texas, were conducted annually by the USGS from 1988 to 1998 and from 2004 to 2013 as part of the monitoring program. Results of studies conducted from 2006 to 2013 are presented in this report.

Seepage investigations were conducted over a period of 1–2 days in February of each year, during low-flow conditions in the non-irrigation season. During the seepage investigations, discharge was measured at sites along the river and at locations where inflows to the river occurred. Discharge-measurement locations in any year included as many as 24 sites along the Rio Grande and as many as 20 inflow sites within the study reach. Outflows from the river did not occur during the seepage investigations.

Computations presented as part of the seepage investigations include net seepage gain or loss, estimation of uncertainty for each measurement, and significance of the computed seepage gain or loss. Net seepage gain or loss was computed for each subreach by subtracting the discharge measured at the upstream location from the discharge measured at the closest downstream location along the river and then subtracting any inflow to the river within the subreach. Individual discharge measurements were assigned a qualitative accuracy rating that represents the percentage of uncertainty in an individual measurement and was based on a subjective evaluation of the measurement made by the hydrographer on the basis of multiple factors that could affect the quality of the measurement. The uncertainty in the measurement of discharge was assigned a numerical value, derived from the qualitative accuracy rating, as follows: excellent, 2 percent; good, 5 percent; fair, 8 percent; and poor, 10 percent. The cumulative measurement uncertainty associated with the computed net seepage gain or loss for each subreach was determined.

Shallow water depths and poor channel conditions, particularly during dry years, can result in increased uncertainties (exceeding 8 percent) in the computation of net seepage gains and losses. An estimated gain or loss was determined to be meaningful when it exceeded the cumulative measurement uncertainty associated with the net seepage computation. For the determination of significance, the net seepage gain or loss and the cumulative measurement uncertainty were normalized to allow for comparison between subreaches with varying discharges and for a particular subreach in different years. The percentage of normalized seepage gain or loss and normalized cumulative uncertainty was computed for each subreach. A computed loss or gain for a subreach was considered meaningful if the percentage of normalized seepage difference was greater than or equal to the percentage of normalized cumulative uncertainty. Study reaches during 2006 to 2013 ranged from 20.2 to 64 miles in length, and seepage losses ranged from 8.2 ± 3.1 to 47.9 ± 8.2 cubic feet per second.

References Cited

Hendricks, E.L., 1964, Compilation of records of surface waters of the United States, October 1950 to September 1960: U.S. Geological Survey Water-Supply Paper 1732, 574 p. (Also available at http://pubs.usgs.gov/wsp/1732/report.pdf.)

Kilpatrick, F.A., and Schneider, V.R., 1983, Use of flumes in measuring discharge: U.S. Geological Survey Techniques of Water-Resources Investigations, book 3, chap. A14, 46 p. (Also available at http://pubs.usgs.gov/twri/twri3-a14/.)

Moyer, D.L., Anderholm, S.K., Hogan, J.F., Phillips, F.M., Hibbs, B.J., Witcher, J.C., Matherne, A.M., and Falk, S.E., 2013, Knowledge and understanding of dissolved solids in the Rio Grande–San Acacia, New Mexico, to Fort Quitman, Texas, and plan for future studies and monitoring: U.S. Geological Survey Open-File Report 2013–1190, 55 p., http://pubs.usgs.gov/of/2013/1190/.

National Climatic Data Center, 2012, Climate Data Online—Quality controlled local climatological data, COOP station 412797, El Paso International Airport, El Paso, TX: National Oceanic and Atmospheric Administration, accessed November 29, 2012, at http://www.ncdc.noaa.gov/cdo-web/.

National Climatic Data Center, 2013, Climate Data Online—Quality controlled local climatological data, COOP station 412797, El Paso International Airport, El Paso, TX: National Oceanic and Atmospheric Administration, accessed April 18, 2013, at http://www.ncdc.noaa.gov/cdo-web/.

Nolan, K.M., and Shields, R.R., 2000, Measurement of stream discharge by wading: U.S. Geological Survey Water-Resources Investigations Report 00–4036, on CD-ROM.

Oberg, K.A., Morlock, S.E., and Caldwell, W.S., 2005, Quality assurance plan for discharge measurements using acoustic Doppler current profilers: U.S. Geological Survey Scientific Investigations Report 2005–5183, 35 p. (Also available at http://pubs.usgs.gov/sir/2005/5183/SIR_2005-5183.pdf.)

Rantz, S.E., and others, 1982, Measurement and computation of streamflow, volume 1—Measurement of stage and discharge: U.S. Geological Survey Water-Supply Paper 2175, 284 p. (Also available at http://pubs.usgs.gov/wsp/wsp2175/.)

Sauer, V.B., and Meyer, R.W., 1992, Determination of error in individual discharge measurements: U.S. Geological Survey Open-File Report 92–144, 21 p. (Also available at http://pubs.usgs.gov/of/1992/ofr92-144/.)

Simonds, F.W., and Sinclair, K.A., 2002, Surface water-ground water interactions along the Lower Dungeness River and vertical hydraulic conductivity of streambed sediments, Clallam County, Washington, September 1999–July 2001: U.S. Geological Survey Water-Resources Investigations Report 02–4161, 60 p.

Turnipseed, D.P., and Sauer, V.B., 2010, Discharge measurements at gaging stations: U.S. Geological Survey Techniques and Methods, book 3, chap. A8, 87 p. (Also available at http://pubs.usgs.gov/tm/tm3-a8/.)

U.S. Geological Survey, 2006, Collection of water samples (ver. 2.0): U.S. Geological Survey Techniques of Water-Resources Investigations, book 9, chap. A4, September 2006, accessed May 22, 2013, at http://pubs.water.usgs.gov/twri9A4/.

U.S. Geological Survey, 2013, USGS Water Science School water science glossary of terms: U.S. Geological Survey, accessed June 7, 2013, at http://ga.water.usgs.gov/edu/dictionary html).

Wheeler, J.D., and Eddy-Miller, C.A., 2005, Seepage investigation on selected reaches of Fish Creek, Teton County, Wyoming, 2004: U.S. Geological Survey Scientific Investigations Report 2005–5133, 20 p. (Also available at http://pubs.usgs.gov/sir/2005/5133/.)

Wilberg, D.E., and Stolp, B.J., 2005, Seepage investigation and selected hydrologic data for the Escalante River drainage basin, Garfield and Kane Counties, Utah, 1909–2002: U.S. Geological Survey Scientific Investigations Report 04–5233, 39 p. (Also available at http://pubs.usgs.gov/sir/2004/5233/PDF/SIR2004_5233.pdf.)

Wilberg, D.E., Swenson, R.L., Slaugh, B.A., Howells, J.H., and Christiansen, H.K., 2001, Seepage investigation for Leap, South Ash, Wet Sandy, and Leeds Creek in the Pine Valley Mountains, Washington County, Utah, 1998: U.S. Geological Survey Water-Resources Investigations Report 01–4237, 42 p.

Wilde, F.D., and Radtke, D.B., eds., variously dated, Field measurements: U.S. Geological Survey National Field Manual for the Collection of Water-Quality Data (Techniques of Water-Resources Investigations, book 9), chap. A6. (Also available at http://water.usgs.gov/owq/FieldManual/Chapter6/Ch6_contents.html.)

Wilkins, D.W., 1986, Geohydrology of the southwest alluvial basins regional aquifer-systems analysis, parts of Colorado, New Mexico, and Texas: U.S. Geological Survey Water-Resources Investigations Report 84–4224, 61 p.

Appendix 1—Select Field Measurements and Observations, Rio Grande Seepage Investigations, 2006–13

Appendix 1.   Select field measurements and observations, Rio Grande seepage investigations, 2006–13.

[ID, identification number; C, degrees Celsius; µS/cm, microsiemens per centimeter; ft³/s, cubic feet per second; ADV, Acoustic Doppler Velocimeter; discharge rating of P, poor, F, fair, G, good, and E, excellent; ——, not applicable; LB, left bank; P-flume, Parshall flume; Reported-I, reported instantaneous discharge; Reported-MDI, reported mean daily instantaneous discharge; PVC, polyvinyl chloride]

Site ID	Sample date	Sample time (military)	Water temperature (°C)	Specific conductance at 25°C (µS/cm)	Instantaneous discharge measurement (ft³/s)	Discharge measurement type	Discharge rating	Streamflow conditions	Channel conditions
1	2/14/2006	945	7.8	1,850	6.67	ADV	G	Channelized LB, laminar flow	Silt, sand, firm.
2	2/14/2006	1130	10.5	1,810	6.92	ADV	G	Channelized LB, laminar flow	Silt, sand, firm.
3	2/14/2006	1212	——	——	0	——	——	No flow	——
4	2/14/2006	1245	10.5	2,060	11.1	ADV	G	Somewhat turbulent just above riffle	Silt, firm.
5	2/14/2006	1430	14.5	1,930	8.65	ADV	G	Slow, fairly uniform	Silt, pebbles, firm.
6	2/14/2006	1500	——	——	0	——	——	No flow	——
7	2/14/2006	930	6.0	1,870	5.57	ADV	G	Slow, steady	Sand, smooth bottom.
8	2/14/2006	1120	9.5	1,880	0.144	P-Flume	E	Flume measurement	Sand, gravel.
9	2/14/2006	1000	18.5	1,310	18.6	Reported-I	F	Metered flow	——
10	2/14/2006	1310	20.0	1,310	10.7	ADV	G	Slow, steady	Smooth sand, gravel covered with algae.
10A	2/14/2006	1353	21.0	1,330	0.03	P-Flume	E	Flume measurement; very slow, suspended algae	Smooth sand, gravel covered with algae.
11	2/14/2006	1415	——	——	0	——	——	No flow	——
12	2/14/2006	1430	——	——	0	——	——	No flow	——
13	2/14/2006	800	——	——	0	——	——	No flow	——
14	2/14/2006	835	——	——	0	——	——	No flow	——
15	2/14/2006	900	——	——	0	——	——	No flow	——
16	2/14/2006	920	——	——	0	——	——	No flow	——
17	2/14/2006	1500	20.9	1,450	0.09	P-Flume	E	Slow	Sand, very shallow.
18	2/14/2006	1050	8.0	1,470	5.32	ADV	G	Steady, clear	Mud, sand, fairly even depth.
18A	2/14/2006	1615	17.0	1,400	0.37	Reported-MDI	P	Metered flow	——
19	2/14/2006	1240	13.5	1,480	5.77	ADV	G	Steady, murky	Sand, firm, fairly even depth.
20	2/14/2006	1450	9.5	2,140	4.05	ADV	F	Steady, clear	Sand, silt, rocky, firm.
21	2/14/2006	1542	13.0	1,800	12.0	ADV	G	Slow, steady, murky	Sand, silt.
22	2/14/2006	1612	16.0	1,760	12.3	ADV	G	Steady, clear	Shifting sand.
22	2/15/2006	920	9.0	1,770	11.5	ADV	G	Slightly deep channelized RB, shallow in middle	Sand, silt, firm.
23	2/15/2006	1135	——	——	0.004	P-Flume	E	Flume measurement was 0.0045	——
24	2/15/2006	900	9.2	2,180	2.28	ADV	F	Channelized, somewhat laminar	Silt, mud, soft.

Appendix 1.   Select field measurements and observations, Rio Grande seepage investigations, 2006–13.—Continued

[ID, identification number; C, degrees Celsius; µS/cm, microsiemens per centimeter; ft³/s, cubic feet per second; ADV, Acoustic Doppler Velocimeter; discharge rating of P, poor, F, fair, G, good, and E, excellent; ——, not applicable; LB, left bank; P-flume, Parshall flume; Reported-I, reported instantaneous discharge; Reported-MDI, reported mean daily instantaneous discharge; PVC, polyvinyl chloride]

Site ID	Sample date	Sample time (military)	Water temperature (°C)	Specific conductance at 25°C (µS/cm)	Instantaneous discharge measurement (ft³/s)	Discharge measurement type	Discharge rating	Streamflow conditions	Channel conditions
25	2/15/2006	1225	14.5	1,880	12.6	ADV	G	Somewhat laminar, deepest on RB	Silt, sand, firm.
25C	2/15/2006	1240	21.5	1,800	2.23	Reported-MDI	P	Well discharge surging	Well inflow (PVC pipe).
26	2/15/2006	1320	17.0	1,830	8.66	ADV	G	Channelized in center, fairly even, slow	——
27	2/15/2006	1415	18.0	1,820	6.14	ADV	G	Somewhat centered, even depths across	Silt, sand, firm, even depth.
28	2/15/2006	920	10.0	1,810	3.40	ADV	F	Slow, clear	Sand, shallow.
29	2/15/2006	1112	12.0	1,850	2.41	ADV	G	Slow, clear	Sand, shallow.
30	2/15/2006	1129	20.0	2,070	2.54	Reported-I	F	Metered flow	——
31	2/15/2006	1138	17.0	1,940	4.59	ADV	G	Suspended algae	Sand, mud, algae, smooth, fairly uniform.
32	2/15/2006	1515	15.5	3,260	16.3	ADV	G	Steady, murky	Silt, sand, firm.
32A	2/15/2006	1450	17.5	4,870	0.573	Reported-MDI	P	Discharge from cooling pond	PVC discharge pipe LB.
33	2/15/2006	1455	18.0	3,650	0.076	P-Flume	E	Flume measurement; steady	——
33A	2/15/2006	1525	17.0	4,360	0.025	P-Flume	E	Flume measurement; steady, clear	Mud, shallow.
34	2/15/2006	1610	17.0	3,690	22.0	ADV	G	Steady, murky	Silt, sand, firm.
1	2/13/2007	900	8.0	1,590	28.7	ADV	F	Fairly even some floating organics, slightly murky	Sand, fairly even some dunes.
2	2/13/2007	1010	8.5	1,590	31.0	ADV	G	Fairly even, floating organics, somewhat murky	Sand, fairly even, some dunes, some boulders.
3	2/13/2007	1106	——	——	0	——	——	No flow	——
4	2/13/2007	1205	10.0	1,670	31.8	ADV	G	Uneven, shallow, floating organics	Sand, uneven, dunes.
5	2/13/2007	1340	11.5	1,630	33.4	ADV	G	Fairly even, murky, lots of floating organics	Mud, fairly even, sand-bar with dunes.
6	2/13/2007	1435	——	——	0	——	——	No flow	——
7	2/13/2007	907	5.0	1,630	18.2	ADV	G	Clear, slow, some debris	Sand, mud, somewhat uniform.
8	2/13/2007	1115	5.0	1,600	20.9	ADV	F	Clear, steady, some debris	Sand, mud.
9	2/13/2007	1415	19.0	1,300	12.9	Reported-I	F	Metered flow	——
10	2/13/2007	1247	9.0	1,490	33.5	ADV	F	Cloudy, steady, suspended debris	Sand, gravel, silt, somewhat uniform.
11	2/13/2007	1645	6.0	1,660	0.069	P-Flume	E	Clear, steady	Mud, fairly uniform.

Appendix 1.   Select field measurements and observations, Rio Grande seepage investigations, 2006–13.—Continued

[ID, identification number; C, degrees Celsius; μS/cm, microsiemens per centimeter; ft³/s, cubic feet per second; ADV, Acoustic Doppler Velocimeter; discharge rating of P, poor, F, fair, G, good, and E, excellent; —, not applicable; LB, left bank; P-flume, Parshall flume; Reported-I, reported instantaneous discharge; Reported-MDI, reported mean daily instantaneous discharge; PVC, polyvinyl chloride]

Site ID	Sample date	Sample time (military)	Water temperature (°C)	Specific conductance at 25°C (μS/cm)	Instantaneous discharge measurement (ft³/s)	Discharge measurement type	Discharge rating	Streamflow conditions	Channel conditions
12	2/13/2007	1535	8.0	1,480	30.3	ADV	G	Cloudy, steady, suspended debris	Mud, sand, soft.
13	2/13/2007	905	6.5	1,500	18.3	ADV	G	Steady, slow, cloudy	Sand, mud, firm.
14	2/13/2007	1020	8.0	1,490	18.1	ADV	G	Steady, cloudy	Firm.
15	2/13/2007	1112	—	—	0	—	—	No flow	—
16	2/13/2007	1225	9.0	1,460	15.0	ADV	G	Steady, slow, cloudy	Sand, firm.
17	2/13/2007	1440	11.5	1,420	13.9	ADV	G	Steady cloudy, deeper on LB	Sand, firm.
17	2/14/2007	840	5.0	1,400	13.4	ADV	G	Slow, clear	Sand, fairly even.
18	2/14/2007	840	7.0	1,400	4.86	ADV	G	Fairly even, steady, murky	Mud, fairly even.
18A	2/14/2007	1400	15.5	1,310	0.388	Reported-MDI	P	Metered flow	—
19	2/14/2007	1005	8.5	1,420	16.3	ADV	G	Fairly even, murky, lots of floating organics	Fairly even, sand dunes.
20	2/14/2007	1115	—	2,100	0.001	P-Flume	E	Dripping out of gate on RB side	—
21	2/14/2007	1145	10.6	1,470	17.1	ADV	F	Fairly even, steady, murky, few floating organics	Sand, even between boulders, dunes.
22	2/14/2007	1625	9.0	1,970	18.8	ADV	G	Fairly clear, deep channel on LB side	Shifting sand.
23	2/14/2007	1720	—	1,440	0.010	P-Flume	G	Clear	Mud.
24	2/14/2007	950	7.5	2,520	3.31	ADV	F	Cloudy, suspended debris	Mud, silt, soft.
25	2/14/2007	1055	7.0	1,550	24.7	ADV	G	Cloudy, steady	Slowly shifting sand.
26	2/14/2007	1230	7.0	1,450	21.4	ADV	G	Fairly clear	Sand, mud.
27	2/14/2007	1415	9.5	1,430	19.3	ADV	G	Steady, slow, somewhat cloudy	Sand, silt, shifting sand.
28	2/14/2007	1025	9.0	1,460	15.6	ADV	G	Slow, steady, cloudy	Sand, mud, firm.
29	2/14/2007	1225	10.5	1,440	12.0	ADV	G	Slow, cloudy	Sand, firm, fairly even.
30	2/14/2007	1513	19.0	2,570	3.01	Reported-I	F	Metered Flow	—
31	2/14/2007	1345	11.0	1,600	14.5	ADV	F	Steady, slow, cloudy	Fairly even.
32	2/14/2007	1505	13.0	3,610	20.8	ADV	G	Steady, cloudy	Firm, fairly even.
32A	2/14/2007	1425	12.5	5,770	0.604	Reported-MDI	P	Discharge from cooling pond	PVC discharge pipe LB.
33	2/14/2007	1630	14.0	730	0.565	ADV	P	Very slow, very murky	Very rocky.
33A	2/14/2007	1450	—	5,050	0.013	P-Flume	E	Even clear	Flume measurement.
34	2/14/2007	1345	12.0	3,020	38.4	ADV	G	Even, very murky, some floating organics	Sand, fairly even.

Appendix 1.   Select field measurements and observations, Rio Grande seepage investigations, 2006–13.—Continued

[ID, identification number; C, degrees Celsius; µS/cm, microsiemens per centimeter; ft³/s, cubic feet per second; ADV, Acoustic Doppler Velocimeter; discharge rating of P, poor, F, fair, G, good, and E, excellent; ——, not applicable; LB, left bank; P-flume, Parshall flume; Reported-I, reported instantaneous discharge; Reported-MDI, reported mean daily instantaneous discharge; PVC, polyvinyl chloride]

Site ID	Sample date	Sample time (military)	Water tempera-ture (°C)	Specific conductance at 25°C (µS/cm)	Instantaneous discharge measurement (ft³/s)	Discharge measurement type	Discharge rating	Streamflow conditions	Channel conditions
1	2/12/2008	1000	8.7	1,680	17.7	ADV	G	Even, steady, some floating organics	Fairly even, some dunes.
2	2/12/2008	1215	12.0	1,680	19.3	ADV	G	Even, steady, lots of floating organics	Fairly even, moss covered rocks to sand.
3	2/12/2008	1255	——	——	0	——	——	No flow	——
4	2/12/2008	1345	0.0	1,790	21.3	ADV	G	Fairly even, steady, floating organics	Sand, moss covered gravel, fairly even, dunes.
5	2/12/2008	1500	6.5	1,740	19.1	ADV	G	Even, steady, some floating organics	Fairly even, dunes.
6	2/12/2008	1551	——	——	0	——	——	No flow	——
7	2/12/2008	1000	5.5	1,760	15.8	ADV	G	Clear, slow	Smooth sand, gravel, fairly even.
8	2/12/2008	1135	12.1	1,800	9.82	ADV	G	Clear, steady, slow	Packed sand and mud, small rocks.
9	2/12/2008	1045	18.5	1,210	17.0	Reported-I	F	Metered flow	——
10	2/12/2008	1420	19.5	1,420	19.4	ADV	G	Algae chunks	Sand.
11	2/12/2008	1550	——	——	0	——	——	No flow	——
12	2/12/2008	1610	19.5	1,560	13.6	ADV	G	Clear, suspended algae chunks	Sand, silt, algae.
13	2/12/2008	900	5.2	1,520	6.10	ADV	F	Slow, steady. Shallow	Sand, firm.
14	2/12/2008	1200	16.0	1,480	6.89	ADV	F	Slow, cloudy	Sand, firm.
15	2/12/2008	1330	——	——	0	——	——	No flow	——
16	2/12/2008	1405	18.0	1,430	2.24	ADV	G	Steady, clear	Sand, fairly even.
17	2/12/2008	1445	19.2	1,350	0.200	ADV	P	Slow, cloudy, shallow	Sand, firm.
17	2/13/2008	815	4.5	1,380	0.736	ADV	P	Slow, clear, shallow, narrow	Sand, firm.
18	2/13/2008	830	6.4	1,330	4.79	ADV	G	Even, steady, clear	Moss covered cement.
18A	2/13/2008	1145	17.0	1,250	0.43	Reported-MDI	P	Metered flow	——
19	2/13/2008	1025	7.5	1,350	5.75	ADV	G	Fairly even, floating organics	Uneven, dunes.
20	2/13/2008	1220	9.0	1,990	2.43	ADV	G	Fairly even, steady, cloudy	Uneven, cobbles to boulders.
21	2/13/2008	1320	14.0	1,630	10.2	ADV	G	Fairly even, steady, cloudy, algae	Sand, fairly even.
22	2/13/2008	1500	18.7	1,480	10.4	ADV	G	Even, steady, cloudy	Uneven, dunes, algae.
23	2/13/2008	1615	11.0	1,610	0.090	P-Flume	F	No flow	——
24	2/13/2008	930	7.3	2,320	2.85	ADV	G	Cloudy	Mud, soft

Appendix 1.   Select field measurements and observations, Rio Grande seepage investigations, 2006–13.—Continued

[ID, identification number; C, degrees Celsius; μS/cm, microsiemens per centimeter; ft³/s, cubic feet per second; ADV, Acoustic Doppler Velocimeter; discharge rating of P, poor, F, fair, G, good, and E, excellent; ——, not applicable; LB, left bank; P-flume, Parshall flume; Reported-I, reported instantaneous discharge; Reported-MDI, reported mean daily instantaneous discharge; PVC, polyvinyl chloride]

Site ID	Sample date	Sample time (military)	Water tempera-ture (°C)	Specific conductance at 25°C (μS/cm)	Instantaneous discharge measurement (ft³/s)	Discharge measurement type	Discharge rating	Streamflow conditions	Channel conditions
25	2/13/2008	1055	7.5	1,750	12.0	ADV	G	Cloudy with organics, mostly algae	Sand, silt
26	2/13/2008	1315	19.4	1,390	9.77	ADV	G	Cloudy	No data.
27	2/13/2008	1505	20.0	1,400	7.31	ADV	G	Cloudy, slow	Sand. Mud, fairly firm.
28	2/13/2008	930	7.9	1,360	3.90	ADV	G	Slow, steady, clear	Sand, firm.
29	2/13/2008	1125	12.5	1,400	0.892	ADV	G	Clear, slow	Sand, firm, even.
30	2/13/2008	1615	19.5	2,280	2.77	Reported-I	F	Metered flow	——
31	2/13/2008	1310	20.5	2,070	2.60	ADV	G	Frothy	Sand, firm, fairly even.
32	2/13/2008	1600	16.4	3,980	15.8	ADV	G	Steady, murky	Mud, silt.
32A	2/13/2008	1500	17.0	6,790	0.130	Reported-MDI	P	Metered flow	PVC discharge pipe LB.
33	2/13/2008	1705	17.0	3,040	0.286	ADV	P	Steady, clear	Narrow, shallow.
33A	2/13/2008	1735	14.0	3,860	0.057	P-Flume	G	Very slow	Very shallow.
34	2/13/2008	1425	17.5	3,760	23.5	ADV	G	Slow, steady, cloudy	Sand, mud, firm, fairly even.
1	2/10/2009	945	4.7	1,660	31.0	ADV	G	Even, steady, clear	Sand, fairly even, dunes.
2	2/10/2009	1120	6.0	1,670	34.5	ADV	G	Even, steady, clear	Fairly even, dunes, shallow in center.
3	2/10/2009	1200	——	——	0	——	——	No flow	——
4	2/10/2009	1305	9.0	1,790	38.2	ADV	G	Even, steady, clear, wind affected	Sand, fairly even, dunes.
5	2/10/2009	1415	9.0	1,760	34.2	ADV	G	Even, steady, clear, wind affected	Sand, fairly even, dunes.
6	2/10/2009	1500	——	——	0	——	——	No flow	——
7	2/10/2009	930	4.0	1,720	34.9	ADV	G	Clear	Sand, soft.
8	2/10/2009	1130	4.8	1,710	28.5	ADV	G	Clear	Sand, rocks on edge.
9	2/10/2009	1130	16.5	1,230	17.5	Reported-I	F	Metered flow	——
10	2/10/2009	1415	11.0	1,570	39.4	ADV	G	Dirty with suspended algae and organics	Uneven, rocks, moss covered sand.
11	2/10/2009	1500	——	——	0	——	——	No flow	——
12	2/10/2009	1535	9.0	1,690	34.9	ADV	G	Cloudy with lots of suspended organics	——
13	2/10/2009	915	4.5	1,610	25.6	ADV	F	Cloudy	Sand, firm, shallow soft RB.
14	2/10/2009	1050	5.0	1,600	24.6	ADV	F	Steady, cloudy	Sand, firm, fairly even.
15	2/10/2009	1135	——	——	0	——	——	No flow	——

Appendix 1.   Select field measurements and observations, Rio Grande seepage investigations, 2006–13.—Continued

[ID, identification number; C, degrees Celsius; µS/cm, microsiemens per centimeter; ft³/s, cubic feet per second; ADV, Acoustic Doppler Velocimeter; discharge rating of P, poor, F, fair, G, good, and E, excellent; ——, not applicable; LB, left bank; P-flume, Parshall flume; Reported-I, reported instantaneous discharge; Reported-MDI, reported mean daily instantaneous discharge; PVC, polyvinyl chloride]

Site ID	Sample date	Sample time (military)	Water tempera-ture (°C)	Specific conductance at 25°C (µS/cm)	Instantaneous discharge measurement (ft³/s)	Discharge measurement type	Discharge rating	Streamflow conditions	Channel conditions
16	2/10/2009	1210	6.0	1,590	17.4	ADV	F	Steady, clear	Sand, shallow, firm.
17	2/10/2009	1330	8.2	1,550	18.0	ADV	G	Steady	Sand, firm.
17	2/11/2009	810	0.0	1,600	15.3	ADV	F	Steady, clear, ice in channels	Fairly even across, ice on banks.
18	2/11/2009	845	1.3	1,370	4.16	ADV	F	Even, steady, cloudy	Fairly even across.
18A	2/11/2009	1130	15.5	1,390	0.480	Reported-MDI	P	Metered flow	——
19	2/11/2009	1005	3.0	1,580	17.9	ADV	G	Even, steady, clear	Fairly even, dunes.
20	2/11/2009	1135	5.5	2,130	4.5	ADV	G	Cloudy, steady, even	Uneven, sand, mud to boul-der, algae.
21	2/11/2009	1225	9.5	1,760	23.2	ADV	G	Even, steady, fairly clear	Fairly even, dunes.
21A	2/11/2009	830	17.5	2,120	1.13	Reported-I	F	Metered flow	——
22	2/11/2009	1415	12.3	1,710	25.9	ADV	F	Steady, cloudy	Fairly even, dunes, split channel.
23	2/11/2009	1555	——	1,710	0.025	P-Flume	G	Even, clear	Flume measure-ment.
24	2/11/2009	830	3.7	2,530	3.27	ADV	P	Murky	Loose mud, soft.
25	2/11/2009	1025	3.5	1,820	30.8	ADV	F	Murky with organic debris	Sand, mud, soft, uneven.
26	2/11/2009	1200	9.7	1,670	26.6	ADV	F	Slow	Sand, mud, soft.
27	2/11/2009	1435	14.0	1,690	23.5	ADV	G	Cloudy with suspend-ed organics	Sand, mud, soft.
28	2/11/2009	1530	13.7	1,620	20.5	ADV	G	Clear with suspended organics	Sand, mud, silt.
29	2/11/2009	950	4.0	1,680	14.1	ADV	G	Steady, clear	Sand, firm.
30	2/11/2009	1415	19.5	2,320	2.42	Reported-I	F	Metered flow	——
31	2/11/2009	1200	9.0	1,800	18.2	ADV	G	Steady, cloudy	Sand, rocks, firm.
32	2/11/2009	1330	12.2	3,760	20.0	ADV	G	Steady, murky	Sand, mud, firm.
32A	2/11/2009	1545	——	——	0	——	——	No flow	——
33	2/11/2009	1510	16.0	4,710	0.576	ADV	P	Very slow	Deep mud, silt, very soft.
33A	2/11/2009	1650	14.0	3,840	0.025	P-Flume	G	Flume	——
34	2/11/2009	1700	13.3	2,910	34.5	ADV	F	Steady	Sand, firm, shal-low.
22	2/23/2010	938	4.8	1,680	12.5	ADV	F	Steady	Sand, soft, un-even.
23	2/23/2010	940	13.5	2,000	0.021	P-Flume	G	Steady, clear	Very shallow, narrow.

Appendix 1.   Select field measurements and observations, Rio Grande seepage investigations, 2006–13.—Continued

[ID, identification number; C, degrees Celsius; µS/cm, microsiemens per centimeter; ft³/s, cubic feet per second; ADV, Acoustic Doppler Velocimeter; discharge rating of P, poor, F, fair, G, good, and E, excellent; ——, not applicable; LB, left bank; P-flume, Parshall flume; Reported-I, reported instantaneous discharge; Reported-MDI, reported mean daily instantaneous discharge; PVC, polyvinyl chloride]

Site ID	Sample date	Sample time (military)	Water temperature (°C)	Specific conductance at 25°C (µS/cm)	Instantaneous discharge measurement (ft³/s)	Discharge measurement type	Discharge rating	Streamflow conditions	Channel conditions
24	2/23/2010	945	7.4	2,370	2.11	ADV	F	Murky, slow, suspended organics	Soft muck, irregular, uneven.
25	2/23/2010	1120	14.0	1,760	12.6	ADV	G	Steady	Sand, firm.
26	2/23/2010	1130	10.5	1,580	11.3	ADV	G	Cloudy	Sand, soft.
27	2/23/2010	1140	11.0	1,610	9.8	ADV	G	Slow, steady, clear	Sand, firm, fairly even.
28	2/23/2010	1305	11.8	1,630	6.2	ADV	G	Steady	Sand, firm, even.
29	2/23/2010	1600	14.5	1,570	3.6	ADV	G	Cloudy	Sand, soft, semi-uniform.
30	2/23/2010	1445	19.3	2,130	2.11	Reported-I	F	Metered flow	——
31	2/23/2010	1325	10.0	1,530	3.77	ADV	G	Steady, clear	Sand, firm, shallow.
32	2/23/2010	1545	15.4	3,390	19.5	ADV	G	Steady	Sand, firm, uneven.
32A	2/23/2010	1515	——	——	0	——	——	No flow	——
33	2/23/2010	1340	17.0	4,190	0.729	P-Flume	G	Murky	Very soft clay.
33A	2/23/2010	1430	14.0	4,250	0.057	P-Flume	G	Steady	Very narrow, shallow.
34	2/23/2010	1535	16.6	3,000	27.7	ADV	F	Steady	Sand, firm.
34A	2/23/2010	1910	8.7	2,930	0.184	P-Flume	E	Steady	Flume measurement.
34B	2/23/2010	1300	20.8	1,880	1.40	ADV	P	Steady	Sand, rocks, soft.
35	2/23/2010	1505	16.5	2,670	8.31	ADV	G	Choppy on RB; steady	Cobble, somewhat even.
36	2/23/2010	1640	27	703	36.4	ADV	G	Steady, fairly even	Mud, soft, even.
22	2/15/2011	945	9	1,840	5.14	P-Flume	F	Steady	Sand, semi-firm, uneven.
23	2/15/2011	905	13.5	1,860	0.010	P-Flume	G	Steady, clear	Very shallow, narrow.
24	2/15/2011	950	5.8	2,260	0.890	ADV	F	Cloudy	Very soft muck.
25	2/15/2011	1100	11.7	1,880	3.41	ADV	G	Steady	Sand, firm, fairly uniform.
26	2/15/2011	1100	——	——	0	——	——	No flow	——
27	2/15/2011	1015	——	——	0	——	——	No flow	——
28	2/15/2011	1030	——	——	0	——	——	No flow	——
29	2/15/2011	1130	——	——	0	——	——	No flow	——
30	2/15/2011	1230	20.1	1,880	2.21	Reported-I	F	Metered flow	——
31	2/15/2011	1127	19.7	1,850	3.26	ADV	F	Steady, cloudy, very slow	Mud, silt.
32	2/15/2011	1330	16.2	3,580	15.6	ADV	G	Steady	Soft, fairly uniform.
32A	2/15/2011	1030	——	——	0	——	——	No flow	——
33	2/15/2011	1230	12.5	3,190	0.533	ADV	F	Cloudy, slow	Muck, silt, soft.

Appendix 1. Select field measurements and observations, Rio Grande seepage investigations, 2006–13.—Continued

[ID, identification number; C, degrees Celsius; µS/cm, microsiemens per centimeter; ft³/s, cubic feet per second; ADV, Acoustic Doppler Velocimeter; discharge rating of P, poor, F, fair, G, good, and E, excellent; ——, not applicable; LB, left bank; P-flume, Parshall flume; Reported-I, reported instantaneous discharge; Reported-MDI, reported mean daily instantaneous discharge; PVC, polyvinyl chloride]

Site ID	Sample date	Sample time (military)	Water tempera-ture (°C)	Specific conductance at 25°C (µS/cm)	Instantaneous discharge measurement (ft³/s)	Discharge measurement type	Discharge rating	Streamflow conditions	Channel conditions
33A	2/15/2011	1315	17.9	3,620	0.045	P-Flume	E	Steady, clear	Mud, silt, soft.
34	2/15/2011	1420	17.8	3,381	17.6	ADV	G	Steady, cloudy	Sand, silt.
34A	2/15/2011	1420	15.3	3,090	0.135	P-Flume	G	Clear	——
35	2/15/2011	1410	21.8	1,940	24.8	ADV	F	Fast, steady, even	Cobble, gravel, hard, even.
36	2/15/2011	1540	20.7	2,620	41.2	ADV	G	Steady, even	Cobble, hard, even.
1	2/28/2012	1015	12.0	3,360	1.31	ADV	F	Steady	Sand, soft.
2	2/28/2012	1215	14.8	3,040	0.866	ADV	F	Steady	Firm, sand.
3	2/28/2012	950	——	——	0	——	——	No flow	——
4	2/28/2012	1015	——	——	0	——	——	No flow	——
5	2/28/2012	1035	——	——	0	——	——	No flow	——
6	2/28/2012	1040	——	——	0	——	——	No flow	——
7	2/28/2012	920	——	——	0	——	——	No flow	——
8	2/28/2012	1011	——	——	0	——	——	No flow	——
9	2/28/2012	945	19.2	1,290	12.7	Reported-I	F	Metered flow	——
10	2/28/2012	920	11.4	1,280	4.37	ADV	F	Steady, slow	Firm, fairly even.
11	2/28/2012	1145	——	——	0	——	——	No flow	——
12	2/28/2012	1148	——	——	0	——	——	No flow	——
13	2/28/2012	1000	——	——	0	——	——	No flow	——
14	2/28/2012	1045	——	——	0	——	——	No flow	——
15	2/28/2012	1124	——	——	0	——	——	No flow	——
16	2/28/2012	1135	——	——	0	——	——	No flow	——
17	2/28/2012	1203	——	——	0	——	——	No flow	——
18	2/28/2012	1120	——	——	0	——	——	No flow	——
18A	2/28/2012	1310	17.5	1,450	0.540	Reported-MDI	P	Metered flow	——
19	2/28/2012	1150	——	——	0	——	——	No flow	——
20	2/28/2012	1155	——	——	0	——	——	No flow	——
21	2/28/2012	1200	——	——	0	——	——	No flow	——
21A	2/28/2012	1430	19.7	2,240	0.535	Reported-I	F	Metered flow	——
22	2/28/2012	1330	——	——	0	——	——	No flow	——
23	2/28/2012	945	15.6	2,020	0.090	P-Flume	F	Flume measurement	——
24	2/28/2012	1400	——	——	0	——	——	No flow	——
25	2/28/2012	1415	——	——	0	——	——	No flow	——
26	2/28/2012	1439	——	——	0	——	——	No flow	——
27	2/28/2012	1256	——	——	0	——	——	No flow	——
28	2/28/2012	1314	——	——	0	——	——	No flow	——
29	2/28/2012	1340	——	——	0	——	——	No flow	——
30	2/28/2012	1140	20.0	2,000	2.14	Reported-I	F	Metered flow	——
31	2/28/2012	1155	18.4	2,020	2.06	ADV	F	Steady	Firm, sand.

Appendix 1. Select field measurements and observations, Rio Grande seepage investigations, 2006–13.—Continued

[ID, identification number; C, degrees Celsius; μS/cm, microsiemens per centimeter; ft³/s, cubic feet per second; ADV, Acoustic Doppler Velocimeter; discharge rating of P, poor, F, fair, G, good, and E, excellent; ——, not applicable; LB, left bank; P-flume, Parshall flume; Reported-I, reported instantaneous discharge; Reported-MDI, reported mean daily instantaneous discharge; PVC, polyvinyl chloride]

Site ID	Sample date	Sample time (military)	Water tempera-ture (°C)	Specific conductance at 25°C (μS/cm)	Instantaneous discharge measurement (ft³/s)	Discharge measurement type	Discharge rating	Streamflow conditions	Channel conditions
32	2/28/2012	1445	15.7	4,310	5.89	ADV	G	Steady	Silt, mud, soft.
32A	2/28/2012	1425	—	—	0	—	—	No flow	—
33	2/28/2012	1345	18.4	3,420	0.412	ADV	P	Slow, steady	Mud, very soft.
33A	2/28/2012	1520	15.9	3,590	0.030	P-Flume	E	Very slow	Very shallow.
34	2/28/2012	1545	17.4	3,820	8.12	ADV	G	Steady	Sand, firm.
34A	2/28/2012	1145	14.8	3,190	0.104	P-Flume	E	Clear	Flume measure-ment.
35	2/28/2012	1315	12.2	2,100	15.3	ADV	F	Clear, steady	Gravel, algae on cobbles, firm, somewhat uniform.
36	2/28/2012	1425	19.5	2,980	22.9	ADV	G	Somewhat clear, steady	Small rocks and cobbles, firm, somewhat uniform.
1	2/26/2013	1015	8	3,220	0.696	ADV	P	Clear, slow shallow	Modified channel to allow 0.3 depth.
2	2/26/2013	1015	5.7	2,680	0.353	ADV	P	—	—
3	2/26/2013	1030	—	—	0	—	—	No flow	—
4	2/26/2013	1034	—	—	0	—	—	No flow	—
5	2/26/2013	808	—	—	0	—	—	No flow	—
6	2/26/2013	800	—	—	0	—	—	No flow	—
7	2/26/2013	1140	—	—	0	—	—	No flow	—
8	2/26/2013	1205	—	—	0	—	—	No flow	—
9	2/26/2013	1315	17.4	1,260	15.8	Reported-I	F	Metered flow	—
10	2/26/2013	1215	13.8	1,320	2.77	ADV	P	Steady; backflow on LB and RB edge.	Uneven.
11	2/26/2013	1400	—	—	0	—	—	No flow	—
12	2/26/2013	1430	—	—	0	—	—	No flow	—
13	2/26/2013	751	—	—	0	—	—	No flow	—
14	2/26/2013	739	—	—	0	—	—	No flow	—
15	2/26/2013	813	—	—	0	—	—	No flow	—
16	2/26/2013	819	—	—	0	—	—	No flow	—
17	2/26/2013	842	—	—	0	—	—	No flow	—
18	2/26/2013	849	—	—	0	—	—	No flow	—
18A	2/26/2013	1055	16.2	1,340	0.480	Reported-MDI	P	Metered flow	—
19	2/26/2013	904	—	—	0	—	—	No flow	—
20	2/26/2013	935	—	—	0	—	—	No flow	—
21	2/26/2013	1500	—	—	0	—	—	No flow	—
21A	2/26/2013	1545	17.3	2,160	0.668	Reported-I	F	Flume measurement	—
22	2/26/2013	1625	—	—	0	—	—	No flow	—

Appendix 1.   Select field measurements and observations, Rio Grande seepage investigations, 2006–13.—Continued

[ID, identification number; C, degrees Celsius; µS/cm, microsiemens per centimeter; ft³/s, cubic feet per second; ADV, Acoustic Doppler Velocimeter; discharge rating of P, poor, F, fair, G, good, and E, excellent; ——, not applicable; LB, left bank; P-flume, Parshall flume; Reported-I, reported instantaneous discharge; Reported-MDI, reported mean daily instantaneous discharge; PVC, polyvinyl chloride]

Site ID	Sample date	Sample time (military)	Water temperature (°C)	Specific conductance at 25°C (µS/cm)	Instantaneous discharge measurement (ft³/s)	Discharge measurement type	Discharge rating	Streamflow conditions	Channel conditions
23	2/26/2013	1645	12.7	1,530	0.025	P-Flume	G	Flume	——
24	2/26/2013	1709	——	——	0	——	——	No flow	——
25	2/26/2013	1715	——	——	0	——	——	No flow	——
26	2/26/2013	1724	——	——	0	——	——	No flow	——
27	2/26/2013	830	——	——	0	——	——	No flow	——
28	2/26/2013	846	——	——	0	——	——	No flow	——
29	2/26/2013	900	——	——	0	——	——	No flow	——
30	2/26/2013	1240	18.9	1,860	2.77	Reported-I	F	Metered flow	——
31	2/26/2013	1325	19.5	1,880	2.42	ADV	F	Steady	Very soft bottom.
32	2/26/2013	1530	15.2	4,410	5.61	ADV	P	Steady flow; Murky water with floating suspended solids.	Soft bottom, some rocks; mostly uneven sand.
32A	2/26/2013	1515	——	——	0	——	——	No flow	——
33	2/26/2013	1045	14.3	3,170	0.358	ADV	F	Slow	Soft mud and silt.
33A	2/26/2013	1629	——	——	0	——	——	No flow	——
34	2/26/2013	1550	16.8	3,621	8.64	ADV	G	Even and steady	Even, soft, sand.
34A	2/26/2013	1200	8.7	3,640	0.170	P-Flume	F	Slow	Grass and mud bottom.
35	2/26/2013	1320	20.7	1,860	11.2	ADV	F	Fast	Firm gravel and cobble bottom.
36	2/26/2013	1415	18.2	2,960	18.5	ADV	P	——	——

Publishing support provided by
Lafayette Publishing Service Center

Crilley and others—Seepage Investigations of the Rio Grande from Below Leasburg Dam to Above American Dam, 2006–13—OFR 2013–1233